Bill Rebiger

MW00565901

Jewish

Culture, Religion, Daily Life
Yesterday and Today

Jaron

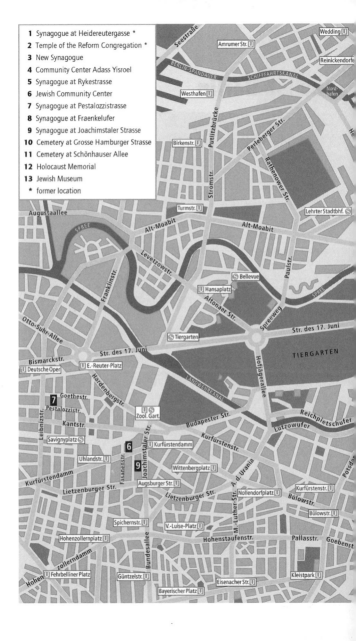

1 Synagogue at Heidereutergasse *
2 Temple of the Reform Congregation *
3 New Synagogue
4 Community Center Adass Yisroel
5 Synagogue at Rykestrasse
6 Jewish Community Center
7 Synagogue at Pestalozzistrasse
8 Synagogue at Fraenkelufer
9 Synagogue at Joachimstaler Strasse
10 Cemetery at Grosse Hamburger Strasse
11 Cemetery at Schönhauser Allee
12 Holocaust Memorial
13 Jewish Museum
* former location

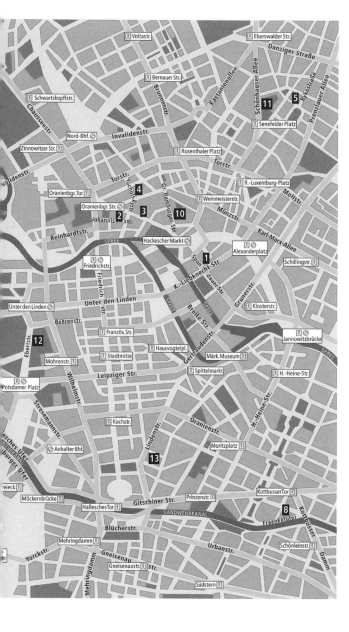

About the Author

Bill Rebiger studied Jewish studies in Berlin and Jerusalem. He received his doctorate in 2004 from the Institute for Jewish Studies at the Freie Universität of Berlin with a dissertation on the magic use of psalms in Judaism. He is currently part of the scholarly staff working on the Jerusalem Talmud research project. He offers tours on Jewish life in Berlin for the association "StattReisen Berlin e. V."

1st Edition 2005
© 2000–2005 Jaron Verlag GmbH, Berlin
(Original title: "Das jüdische Berlin. Kultur, Religion und Alltag gestern und heute")
Translation: Miriamne Fields, Berlin, Paul Bowman, Berlin
Photography: Günter Schneider, Berlin
Map p. 2/3: Matthias Frach, Berlin
Cover design: LVD GmbH, Berlin, using a photograph by Günter Schneider (New Synagogue)
Typography: hanseatenSatz-bremen, Bremen
Repro: LVD GmbH, Berlin
Printed and bound by: Clausen & Bosse, Leck
ISBN 3-89773-099-5

Contents

Jewish Cemeteries

The Shoah – Memorials and Monuments

Cultural Institutions and Events

Jewish Restaurants and Shops

Index of Persons

About this Book

The growing interest in the history, tradition and culture of Jews in Berlin is very apparent at the moment. Anyone interested in Judaism will soon come across the significance of Jewish figures and institutions in Berlin. Anyone exploring Berlin will encounter numerous traces of Jewish life. Anyone who deals with German history will inevitably have to confront the Shoah that began in Berlin.

Jewish life in Berlin has begun to flourish again, especially in the last few years. The number of Jewish community members has doubled to 12,000 in just about ten years as a result of the large number of Jews immigrating to Germany from the former Soviet Union. Despite this positive development it must not be forgotten that the number of Jewish community members living in Berlin today is only about ten percent of the Jewish community that existed before the war. The loss of a Jewish presence, as a result of murder and expulsion organized by people in Germany, is still painfully felt today.

This guidebook presents the sites of Jewish history in Berlin and the most important Jewish figures of the city, and it elucidates the historical and cultural contexts.

The book could not have been written without the help of countless people who offered their criticism and comments. I would particularly like to thank the competent tour guides of the association "Statt-Reisen Berlin e. V.," who provided me with invaluable insight into the past and present of Berlin and its residents. I owe a very special thanks to Katrin Rebiger, who supported me as wife, theologian and pedagogue. Not least of all, my thanks goes to our son Simon Philipp, who, with his tireless curiosity, repeatedly encouraged us to take walks together and explore the fascinating city of Berlin.

Buildings for which there is no longer any structural remains have been marked with an asterisk (*). The simplified transcription of Hebrew terms is presented without diacritical marks and is oriented towards the pronunciation of English-speaking readers.

Chronological Table on the History of the Jews in Berlin

From the Beginning to the Execution of the Mintmaster Lippold

10th c.	The first documented mention of Jews in the Brandenburg region.
13th c.	In Spandau, which is still separate from Berlin, a Jewish cemetery is established where Berlin Jews are also buried. The Jews in Berlin probably did not have their own cemetery at that time.
October 28, 1295	In the guild charter of Berlin wool weavers, guild members are forbidden from buying yarn from Jews. Jews are not allowed to become members of the artisan guilds.
April 5, 1317	In an official document, Margrave Waldemar confirms that the Jews in the twin city of Berlin/Cölln have only to answer to the city magistrate concerning legal issues. They are no longer subordinate to the ruler.
1347–49	After Jews are accused of causing the rampant plague in Berlin and Brandenburg, pogroms break out and Jews are expelled from the area.
1354	Jews are once again permitted to settle in Berlin.
1446	Under the Elector Friedrich II Jews are again expelled from the Brandenburg region. They are re-admitted after Stefan Bodeker, the bishop of Brandenburg, protests.
February 6, 1510	After the Christian tinker Paul Fromm steals a gilded monstrance and two consecrated Hosts from the church in Knoblauch (Havelland), Jews are accused of desecrating the host. Fifty-one Jews are arrested. The tin-

	ker had "confessed" under torture to having given the Host to the Jews.
July 19, 1510	After being found guilty, thirty-nine Jews are publicly burned at the stakes at the New Market in front of St. Mary's Church in Berlin. Afterwards, all Jews are banished from the Brandenburg region and the Spandau cemetery is destroyed.
1539	At the Elector congress of Frankfurt, Josel of Rosheim, the political leader of the German Jews, proves the innocence of the Jewish martyrs of 1510. The Jews are again permitted to settle in Berlin under Elector Joachim II for 42,000 Thaler and the payment of an annual protection fee.
1543	Michael of Derenburg near Halberstadt is appointed Court Jew of the Elector. He is the first known Court Jew in Berlin. Court Jews are privileged Jews who serve their own ruler and are above all responsible for raising the funds needed to maintain the exorbitant courtly lifestyle.
1556	Lippold of Prague is appointed head of the Brandenburg Jews and responsible for inspecting their wealth and collecting their taxes.
1565	Lippold becomes the Elector's mintmaster and is thus responsible for collecting and administrating the general taxes.
January 3, 1571	After the death of Joachim II, Lippold is arrested and charged with poisoning his patron and misappropriating his money. Riots break out against Jews, their homes are plundered and the first Jews are driven out.
1573	After mintmaster Lippold is publicly executed, Elector Johann Georg I demands that all Jews from the Brandenburg region be fined and driven out.

From the Founding of the Jewish Community of Berlin to the Prussian Emancipation Edict

1665	The Court Jew Israel Aaron is granted permission to reside in Berlin. He is responsible for arranging funds for the Great Elector Friedrich Wilhelm's costly plans. Following the devastation of the Thirty Years' War, the ruler hopes to achieve an economic upswing and increase the population by encouraging foreigners and persecuted people to settle in the state.
May 21, 1671	Friedrich Wilhelm approves the edict which allows for fifty prosperous Jewish families that were expelled from Vienna to settle in the Brandenburg region under the condition that they pay an annual protection fee. The letter of protection is at first only valid for twenty years: it is not intended that the Jews settle permanently. Synagogues may not be built, but religious services in private prayer rooms are tolerated.
September 10, 1671	The Jewish Community of Berlin is officially founded.
1672	Property is purchased on Grosse Hamburger Strasse for a Jewish cemetery.
1700	The congregation has approximately seventy members.
1703	A Jewish hospital for the poor opens. It is necessary due to the rapidly rising number of impoverished Jews without a letter of protection.
May 20, 1714	The Edict of 1671 that guarantees Jews the right to residency is confirmed, putting an end to the uncertain legal status of the Berlin Jews that existed during the first decades in which they were allowed to settle here. Jews are no longer under constant threat of expulsion when the protection fee is not paid or

	when a community member engages in illegal conduct.
September 14, 1714	The first synagogue of Berlin in Heidereutergasse is dedicated.
September 29, 1730	In the "General Privileges and Rules", the rights granted in 1714, are to a large degree retracted.
1737	The number of Jews permitted to settle in Berlin is limited to 120 families; 584 propertyless Jews are expelled from the city.
1743	The fourteen year old Moses Mendelssohn arrives in Berlin completely penniless. In the same year approximately 1,945 Jews from 333 families are registered in Berlin.
April 17, 1750	Friedrich II's "Revised General Privileges" imposes an additional restriction on Jews. On the request of the Jewish community, the law is not published until 1756. It distinguishes between six groups of Jews, the top three of which must pay all the taxes and dues.
1778	The enlightened ideas of Moses Mendelssohn find expression in the Jewish Free School founded by David Friedländer, Naphtali Herz Wessely and Isaak Daniel Itzig.
March 11, 1812	Through the Emancipation Edict, Jews of Prussia are declared equal citizens. They are also granted the right to commercial freedom, to reside where they choose, to pursue an academic career and fill local public posts. The edict is for the most part retracted following the Congress of Vienna.

From Reform Jewry to the Emancipation of the Jews in the German Empire

1815	Israel Jacobson and Jacob Herz Beer conduct religious services in Berlin in German with

	a sermon, choir accompaniment and organ music.
1819	Leopold Zunz and Eduard Gans found the Jewish Association for Culture and Science for scholarly research on Judaism.
1822	The Jews are again denied the right to fill high level military posts or academic and school teaching positions.
1823	On the initiative of the orthodox Jews, Friedrich Wilhelm III prohibits all changes in language and ceremony of religious services, leading many reform-oriented Jews to convert.
1826	A Jewish community boys' school is founded.
1826	The Jewish cemetery on Schönhauser Allee opens.
1835	A girls' school is founded.
May 1845	The Berlin Society for Reform in Judaism is founded by Sigismund Stern. The society is later renamed the Jewish Reform congregation, but is not recognized as a separate independent congregation.
1847	The Jewish congregations, which had previously been only "tolerated religious societies", are recognized as public bodies and granted administrative autonomy. They are permitted to run public schools, request state funding for educational institutions and collect taxes from the congregation.
January 31, 1850	The legal equality of all Prussians, including Jews, is set in Article 4 of the revised Prussian constitution. Nevertheless, Jews are still denied access to public posts, high level military positions and university academic chairs.
September 1854	The Temple of the Jewish Reform congregation at Johannisstrasse is dedicated.
September 5, 1866	The liberal New Synagogue (Neue Synagoge) on Oranienburger Strasse is dedicated.

June 1869	Founding of the separate orthodox congregation "Orthodox Jewish religious society Adass Yisroel", which becomes an independent Jewish community in 1885.
July 3, 1869	The North German Confederation, founded in 1867, passes the law on the equal rights of religious confession which declares the emancipation of the Jews within its territory.
April 1871	The North German Confederation's law of 1869 is adopted by the Reich law of the newly founded German Empire.

From Flourishing German Jewry to the End of the Weimar Republic

1872	The private College for the Science of Judaism (Hochschule für die Wissenschaft des Judentums) is founded in Berlin by Moritz Lazarus and Salomon Neumann, after efforts to establish this discipline at the university fail.
October 22, 1873	The orthodox Rabbinical Seminary in Berlin is founded by Esriel Hildesheimer, the rabbi and spiritual leader of the Adass Yisroel congregation.
1875	The Jewish community has 65,000 members.
July 28, 1876	The Law of Withdrawal is passed, allowing Jews to withdraw their membership from the Jewish community without having to convert. It also enables the Adass Yisroel association to withdraw from the Berlin community that same year. In September 1885 Adass Yisroel is officially accepted as an independent religious congregation.
September 9, 1880	The Jewish Cemetery of the main community opens in Weissensee.
1893	The Central Union of German Citizens of the Jewish Faith (Central-Verein deutscher Staatsbürger jüdischen Glaubens) is founded to

	fight increasing antisemitism and to support the recognition of Jews as German citizens.
1910	144,043 Jewish residents are registered in Greater Berlin.
1914–18	More than 12,000 Jewish soldiers die in World War I. At the end of 1916 demands of anti-Semites are conceded to and a so-called "Jew census" is conducted to examine how many Jewish soldiers are fighting at the front. The census finds that the percentage of Jews in the military far outnumbered their representation in the population, but the results are never published.
January 1919	Founding of the Reich Confederation of Jewish Front Soldiers (Reichsbund jüdischer Frontsoldaten) in Berlin, which tries to disprove the accusation that Jews were shirking their duty to serve at the front and aims to defend Jews against antisemitic assaults.
November 5, 1923	Antisemitic riots break out in the Berlin Scheunenviertel.
1925	172,672 Jewish residents are registered in Greater Berlin making up 4.3 percent of the Berlin population. Jewish citizens are less than one percent of the overall German population.
1932	Ninety-four synagogues and temples exist in Berlin.

From the Expulsion of German Jews to the Annihilation of European Jewry

1933	The Jewish community has 160,000 members when the National Socialists come to power under Adolf Hitler.
April 1, 1933	The National Socialists call for a boycott of shops owned by German citizens of the Jewish faith and of Jewish origins.

April 7, 1933	The Law for the Restoration of the Professional Civil Service demands that "civil servants who are not of Aryan origins" be forced to retire. Jews who fought at the front during World War I are exempted until 1935.
July 6, 1933	Founding of the Cultural Union of German Jews (Kulturbund deutscher Juden) that provides Jewish musicians and actors the chance to perform for a Jew audience.
September 17, 1933	Founding of the National Representation of German Jews (Reichsvertretung der deutschen Juden) that is forced in 1939 to change its name to the National Association of Jews in Germany (Reichsvereinigung der Juden in Deutschland) since, according to National Socialism, German Jews cannot exist. In the years to come, the National Association establishes a Jewish school system and founds a number of aid organizations.
September 15, 1935	The "Nuremberg Laws" are passed at the NSDAP national party convention. Racial and pseudo-biological criteria are used to define and classify "Jews" and to determine how Jewish a person is. The "Reich Citizen Law" denies the Jews their political rights. The "Law for Protection of German Blood and Honor" is used to discriminate and defame the so-called "Jewish race."
March 28, 1938	The Jewish communities are denied the status of a public body. They are henceforth treated as private organizations.
October 5, 1938	Passports of German Jews are now marked with a "J."
October 27–28, 1938	During the "Poland Action", 18,000 Polish Jews are arrested and deported to Poland.
November 9–10, 1938	In "retaliation" for the assassination of the diplomat Ernst vom Rath, an employee of

the German embassy in Paris, by the seventeen year old Jew Herschel Grynszpan, Reich Minister of Propaganda Goebbels calls for a nationwide pogrom that is euphemistically called "Reichskristallnacht" (Night of Broken Glass). During this night 191 synagogues in Germany are completely destroyed and another seventy-six are ravaged. Over the following days more than 20,000 Jewish citizens are arrested; most of them are interned in concentration camps. The Jewish community is required to repair the damages and pay a fine of a billion Reich Marks.

1939	Circa 80,000 Jews still live in Berlin. The immigration of German Jews has reached its pinnacle. Approximately 90,000 Jews from Berlin successfully emigrate by 1941.
December 1939	The Gestapo disbands the Adass Yisroel congregation.
September 15, 1941	Jews must be identified by wearing a yellow star.
October 18, 1941	The first deportations from Berlin mark the beginning of the systematic genocide of German Jews. Before the war ends, 55,000 Berlin Jews are deported on sixty-three transports.
January 20, 1942	At the Wannsee Conference, the so-called "Final Solution to the Jewish Question" is resolved and its logistics planned. At this point 58,637 Jews still live in Berlin.
May 18, 1942	The Herbert Baum Jewish-Communist Resistance Group sets the propaganda exhibit in the Berlin Lustgarten on fire. Almost all the group's members are denounced and executed in Plötzensee soon thereafter. The National Socialists retaliate by murdering another 500 Jews from Berlin.

July 7, 1942	All Jewish schools and educational institutions are closed down.
January 28, 1943	The Berlin Jewish community is disbanded.
February 27, 1943	During what is known as the "Factory Action," Jewish forced laborers are arrested at their work sites and held captive at collection sites. They are supposed to be deported to the mass death camps in the East. On Rosenstrasse hundreds of "Aryan" wives protest in a spontaneous demonstration.
June 10, 1943	The National Association of Jews in Germany is disbanded; its remaining assets are confiscated and its last staff members are deported.
March 1945	The last deportation train departs from Berlin.

From the Re-Emergence of Jewish Life in Berlin to the Collapse of the GDR

May 1945	Only about 6,500 Berlin Jews survive, either in so-called "mixed marriages", at the Jewish hospital in the Wedding district, at the Weissensee Jewish cemetery or by living illegally underground. Only 2,000 Jews return to Berlin from the concentration camps. About 200,000 East European Jews move to Germany in order to immigrate from there to the United States or Israel. They are placed in "Displaced Persons" camps that are set up by the Americans. The first Jewish religious services are conducted.
December 20, 1945	The new Jewish community administration in Berlin, headed by Hans-Erich Fabian, officially begins its work. The community differs strongly from the liberal pre-war community as a consequence of the immigration of a large number of very religious East European Jews.

February 1946	The Jewish community is again recognized as a public body.
1949	Heinz Galinski becomes chairman of the Jewish Community of Berlin (from 1953 to 1989 only for West Berlin) and remains so until his death on July 19, 1992.
December 9, 1952	The Union of Jewish congregations in the GDR is recognized by the East German government as a public body.
January 19, 1953	As a result of intense antisemitic persecution in East Germany, many members of the Jewish community flee to the western part of the city or to West Germany. The west and east congregations are administratively divided.
November 1955	The Jewish Cemetery of the West Berlin community opens on Heerstrasse.
September 27, 1959	The Jewish community center on Fasanenstrasse is dedicated. In this center of Jewish life a "vanishing community" evolves into an enduring permanent institution in West Berlin.
1962	The Jewish Adult Education Program (Jüdische Volkshochschule) is established at Fasanenstrasse.
1963	The Union of Jewish congregations in the GDR is excluded from the Central Council of Jews in Germany.
January 1, 1971	An "agreement to regulate issues of mutual interest" is established between the Jewish community (West) and the Berlin Senate.
September 10, 1971	A ceremony is held to celebrate the 300th anniversary of the founding of the Jewish Community of Berlin.
July 4, 1988	Founding of the Berlin New Synagogue – Centrum Judaicum Foundation. The East Berlin community has barely 200 members. For reasons of international policy, the GDR

	starts a campaign to support Jewish institutions. The West Berlin community has about 6,000 members and is once again the largest Jewish community in Germany.
November 9, 1988	The 50th anniversary of the pogrom night of 1938 is remembered by both Berlin communities.
December 18, 1989	Adass Yisroel is recognized again by the GDR government.

The Re-Emergence of Jewish Community Life since German Reunification

1990	The two Berlin Jewish communities are united.
1991	The federal government approves refugee status to Jews from the former Soviet Union. Since then more than 50,000 Jews have immigrated to Germany. By 1997 the number of congregation members in Berlin doubled to about 11,000.
August 26, 1992	After Galinski dies, Jerzy Kanal becomes chairman of the Jewish Community of Berlin.
May 7, 1995	Re-dedication of the reconstructed New Synagogue on Oranienburger Strasse.
June 1997	Andreas Nachama becomes the new chairman of the Jewish Community of Berlin.
October 15, 1997	Following a long and drawn out trial, the Adass Yisroel congregation is recognized as a public body by the Federal Administrative Court.
January 1999	The Jewish Museum building is completed. It opens with a permanent exhibition on September 13, 2001.
June 25, 1999	The German Bundestag resolves to erect the "Memorial for the Murdered Jews of Europe" (Holocaust Memorial) according to a design by Peter Eisenman.

May 2, 2001	Alexander Brenner becomes the new chairman of the Jewish Community of Berlin.
January 7, 2004	Albert Meyer becomes the new chairman of the Jewish Community of Berlin.

The Jewish Community of Berlin is a public body and recognized as a leading association of independent charity work. With 12,000 members, two-thirds of which come from the Soviet Union, it is the largest Jewish community in Germany. Two rabbis representing different currents of religious thought are presently employed by the community. The budget of the community is derived from congregation taxes, donations, service fees and public subsidies.

Synagogues and Community Centers

RELIGIOUS RITUALS

The Greek word "synagogue" literally means "assembly." The Hebrew term for synagogue is *Bet Knesset* meaning "assembly house." A synagogue is also a kind of community center where people come together, discuss community issues, study the holy scriptures and pray together. But a synagogue does not have to be an independent building, it can be established in any room.

The Torah ark is situated behind a beautifully embroidered curtain (*Parokhet* in Hebrew) in a niche in the wall and is ideally facing east to symbolize the direction of Jerusalem. The Torah scrolls are preserved inside the ark. The Eternal Lamp (*Ner Tamid* in Hebrew) burns in front of the ark. A speaker's pulpit (*Bimah* or *Almemor* in Hebrew) for reading the Torah is elevated by a few steps and forms the centerpiece of the room of worship. Later, in Reform Judaism, the speaker's pulpit was placed in front of the Torah ark. Men and women traditionally sit in separate areas. In larger synagogues there is a balcony where the women sit. The synagogue room is usually decorated with Jewish symbols such as the Star of David, the seven-armed candelabra (*Menorah* in Hebrew), the two covenant tablets with the ten commandments, lions to signify the strength of wisdom and Hebrew letters.

In Judaism there is a ritualized dress code during any religious act in the synagogue, men must wear a head covering (*Kippah* in Hebrew). This also applies to guests, who can usually borrow a simple paper *Kippah* at the entrance.

Jewish religious services consist of prayer and scripture readings. At least ten adult Jewish men (*Minyan* in Hebrew) must be present. In large congregations, either a singer (*Hazan* in Hebrew), also known as a cantor, or a rabbi leads the services. Both official figures are not obligatory since any other congregation member can also fulfill their duties in the services. In principle, religious services are held three times a day – in the morning, afternoon and evening – but the afternoon and evening services are usually combined into a single service. In most of the synagogues in Berlin, services only take place on the Sabbath: Friday evening and Saturday morning.

The large congregation synagogues are presented below in chronological order based on the date of their construction.

SYNAGOGUE AT HEIDEREUTERGASSE *

Lawn next to Rosenstrasse (Mitte)

The building of a synagogue was explicitly forbidden by the Edict of 1671. The first religious services therefore took place in private rooms. In 1708 the Jewish community demanded a building permit for a public synagogue. In 1712 the foundation stone was laid for the synagogue on Heidereutergasse. The synagogue was dedicated on September 14, 1714, on the Sabbath before the Jewish new year.

The Christian architect **Michael Kemmeter** designed the Baroque building. It was at the time considered the most magnificent synagogue in all of Germany. The simple structure, consisting of a single central hall, had a hipped roof without a tower or dome so that it would not be mistaken for a Christian church. Inside, there was a striking carved Baroque Torah ark. The women sat apart from the men on two balcony levels. On April 20, 1718, the Prussian King Friedrich Wilhelm I and his son, the later Friedrich II, visited the synagogue and brought a precious curtain (*Parokhet* in Hebrew) for the Torah ark as a gift.

David Fränkel, Moses Mendelssohn's teacher, was the most famous rabbi of this synagogue. He established a house of study (*Bet ha-Midrash* in Hebrew) in the extension that was added in 1745.

In 1856 the synagogue was renovated and rebuilt in the Classical style by the Christian architect **Eduard Knoblauch**. After the New Synagogue was erected on Oranienburger Strasse in 1866, the synagogue on Heidereutergasse was henceforth referred to as the Old Synagogue.

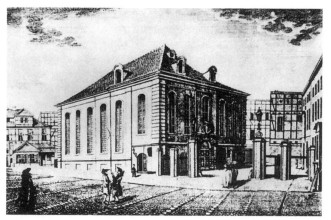

Synagogue at Heidereutergasse, etching by F. A. Calau

Synagogue at Rykestrasse

In the November pogrom of 1938 this house of worship was heavily damaged by rampaging SA hordes. The German Reich post office became the new owners in the same year. Religious services nevertheless still continued to be conducted in the synagogue until 1942. It was destroyed by bombs during World War II and the ruins were torn down in 1960, although the synagogue could have been rebuilt.

An illustrated panel with information in different languages was erected in September 2000, unfortunately it is rather hidden from view. There is also a new wall representing a corner of the former synagogue that gives an impression of the building's original outline. The new street approaching the site was named Heidereutergasse in order to re-establish this street name in the city.

TEMPLE OF THE REFORM CONGREGATION *

Johannisstrasse 16 (Mitte)

Moses Mendelssohn's students and intellectual heirs tried to reform traditional religious services. They wanted to show that Jews also had found a connection to the modern developments of the Christian world in religious concerns as well. It was hoped that cultural assimilation would reinforce Jewish demands for equal civil rights. The first attempt to hold religious services in German took place in 1815 in the home of the banker **Jacob Herz Beer** (1769–1825), the father of the composer Giacomo Meyerbeer. On the insistence of the Orthodox rabbis of the Berlin Jewish community, the Prussian king forbid all changes to religious services in 1823.

Finally, in May 1845, the time was ripe for a second attempt to reform Jewish religious services. It was to this end that **Sigismund Stern** (1812–1867) and **Aaron Bernstein** (1812–1884) founded the Society for Reform in Judaism. The Jewish Reform congregation that later followed was strongly oriented to Protestant liturgy and religious services. Most of the prayers, songs and sermons were performed entirely in German. Passages referring to the return to the land of Israel were omitted. Since prayers were spoken but no longer sung, there was no further need of a cantor. Holiday services, found to be too long, were considerably shortened. Worshippers wore neither skull cap, phylactery nor tallis. The men and women sat together and prayed together. Organ music and mixed choir accompaniment were added. In place of the *Bar Mitswah* – the celebration for thirteen year old boys – a confirmation celebration for both boys and girls was introduced. The *Shofar* was no longer blown on the Day of Atonement. And as of 1849, the main services were only conducted on Sundays. The members of the Reform congregation continued to be members of the main congregation because the struggle to establish the legal independence of the Reform congregation failed. With the liberalization of the main congregation and its adoption of some changes, the Reform congregation became a minority.

The temple was consecrated on a Sunday (!) in September 1854. It was intentionally called a temple to express the claim that the Reform synagogue was the legitimate successor to the destroyed temple in Jerusalem.

The architect **Gustav Stier** (1807–1880) designed the temple in the round arch style of Berlin churches. The ground plan of the synagogue was shaped like a cross and set back from the street. The speaker's pulpit, the *Almemor*, was shifted away from the center to the east. An organ was built into the wall above the Torah ark.

Samuel Holdheim (1806–1860) became its first rabbi as of 1847: He had been influential in Frankfurt/Oder and Schwerin and a driving force behind the Reform movement. His radical credo was: "In the era of the Talmud, the Talmud was right. In my era, I am right."

The synagogue was devastated during the November pogrom of 1938. It was, however, repaired and in April 1940 became the main synagogue of the Berlin community, replacing the New Synagogue on Oranienstrasse that had been taken over by the Wehrmacht. In World War II the Temple of the Reform congregation was destroyed by aerial bombs and torn down after the war.

NEW SYNAGOGUE

Oranienburger Strasse 29 (Mitte), Tel. 345 43 64
Services: Friday 6 pm in winter and 7 pm in summer, Saturday 10 am,
Thursday 7:30 am

NEW SYNAGOGUE OF BERLIN – CENTRUM
JUDAICUM FOUNDATION

Oranienburger Strasse 29 (Mitte), Tel. 284 01–250
Open: Sunday–Thursday 10 am–5:30 pm, Friday 10 am–1:30 pm

The gilded cupola of the New Synagogue can be seen from quite a distance hovering over the roofs of the Spandauer Vorstadt in Berlin-Mitte. Today it is a city landmark as it had been at the time of its construction. And once again a number of Jewish community institutions, restaurants, cafés and the Jewish Gallery are located in the immediate vicinity of the synagogue. This is, however, in no way comparable to the many Jewish synagogues, old age homes, hospitals, schools, nursery schools, shops, restaurants, administrative offices, clubs and organizations that had once made this area a center of Jewish life before the war.

Most people who see the facade of the New Synagogue on the Oranienburger Strasse for the first time are amazed by the unusual architectural style that recalls the Islamic buildings of the Iberian Peninsula.

The rapid growth of the Berlin Jewish community, in particular due to immigration from the East, made it necessary to build a larger synagogue by the mid-19th century. A difficult angular lot on Oranienburger Strasse 30 that already belonged to the community was selected as the building site. A competition for the design of the synagogue was conducted in April 1857 under the chairmanship of the architect **Eduard Knoblauch** (1801–1861). Because no satisfying design was found, Knoblauch was commissioned himself. Since he was responsible for overseeing both the construction of the new building for the Jewish hospital and the renovation of the synagogue on Heidereutergasse, he recommended himself to the community as architect. After he fell seriously ill, Knoblauch was replaced by his colleague Friedrich August Stüler (1800–1865) in 1859. Construction began in May and the topping out ceremony took place as early as July 1861. But its completion was considerably delayed due to the elaborate interior furnishings and a shortage of materials during the war. The building was finally inaugurated on September 5, 1866 in the presence of the Prussian Prime Minister Otto von Bismarck.

The largest synagogue in Germany seated 1,800 men and 1,200 women. Jews and non-Jews alike were delighted by its colorful and decorative interior, the sophisticated lighting system and technically daring iron vault structures. The New Synagogue soon became a Berlin landmark and an architectural monument. It was the largest, most expensive, most prestigious German synagogue ever to be built.

The Hebrew inscription above the portals comes from the biblical prophet Isaiah and reads in English: "Open the gates to let a righteous nation enter, a nation that keeps faith." With its built-in organ, German language services, and accompanying choir, the New Synagogue became a center of Reform Judaism. While it also attracted many non-Jewish visitors with its splendor, it remained a thorn in the eye of Orthodox circles of the Jewish community.

Louis Lewandowski became cantor in the New Synagogue in 1866. He composed his own liturgy for the Liberal services of the New Synagogue and numerous works for choir and organ. Public concerts organized outside the times of services was also new and non-Jewish visitors were naturally welcome. The concerts were usually performed for a good cause. On January 29, 1930, during one of the synagogue concerts conducted by Hermann Jadlowker, two violin duets by Handel and Bach were performed. The soloists were Albert Einstein (1879–1955) and Alfred Lewandowski, the son of Louis Lewandowski.

During the pogrom night of November 9, 1938 the district police chief **Wilhelm Krützfeld** (1880–1953) was able to drive away arsonists by declaring that the synagogue had been placed under protection as a landmark and calling the fire department. Although it could not be shown that he had committed any professional misdemeanor he was punished for his courageous behavior and removed from his post. A memorial plaque on the facade of the New Synagogue honors Krützfeld, who died in Berlin 1953.

Services continued to be held in the synagogue from April 1939 to March 1940. After that the Wehrmacht used it as a storage place for uniforms. Allied bombings on the night of November 22, 1943 severely damaged the building and the ensuing fire gutted it. In the summer of 1958 the destroyed main hall of the synagogue was torn down. The reason why is to this day not known. Only the front part of the building, the soot-blackened domeless ruin, remained. A memorial plaque dated September 5, 1966 still hangs on the facade today.

On July 4, 1988 the **New Synagogue Berlin – Centrum Judaicum Foundation** was founded. The foundation is a city institution and legally independent from the Jewish community. Dr. **Hermann Simon**, author of various publications on the history of the synagogue and the former Jewish Museum next door, and also author of the informative and richly-illustrated permanent exhibition catalogue of the New Synagogue, has served as director of the foundation since its founding.

The foundation was originally established to restore the remaining part of the New Synagogue so that it could be used as a Jewish community center and exhibition space. Erich Honecker, head of the GDR at the time, was present during the laying of the foundation stone on November 10, 1988. The East German government's sudden interest in synagogues and Jewish cemeteries had to do with foreign policy: Honecker was interested in paying a state visit to the United States to improve his international reputation and attain better trade conditions. In a major calculated campaign for the upcoming 50th anniversary of the 1938 November pogrom, Honecker hoped to win over the so-called American "Jewish lobby" for his interests.

The New Synagogue was not completely rebuilt – only the building section facing the street where the lobby and administrative offices of the community had once been located. The main dome and the two corners towers which are also crowned with onion domes were restored to look exactly as they had before. The topping-off ceremony took place on October 29, 1990. Since June 1991 a gilded Star of David glitters above the circa fifty meter high dome. Construction was completed on May 7, 1995 with a ceremonial re-dedication. The remnants of the old building structure and the reconstructed additions have been made clearly visible in many places. The permanent exhibition is located on the ground floor. The upper floor contains a spacious hall that is used for changing exhibitions, ceremonies, lectures and podium discussions.

A small eighty-seat prayer hall where egalitarian services are held was opened in 1998. Men and women sit together and the services are arranged according to the principle of equal rights. The female cantor **Avitall Gerstetter** is employed by the community to lead the services with her lovely voice.

The elaborately restored vestibule, stairwell and former representational hall convey an impression of the earlier decorative interior. The completely glassed back facade opens onto an empty area where the main hall of the synagogue once stood. Eight marble columns mark the site where the Torah ark used to be.

The permanent exhibition features documents, pictures and objects on the history of the synagogue, its partial reconstruction and the Jewish local history, in particular the nearby Spandauer Vorstadt. A few objects found during the restoration work, including the Eternal Lamp, are also on display.

The new building next door at Oranienburger Strasse 29 was completed in July 1993. This building houses offices and the Jewish Adult Education Program. The community's library that was also established here in 1977 had to close at the beginning of 2002.

SYNAGOGUE AT LINDENSTRASSE 48–50 (KREUZBERG) *

The synagogue on Lindenstrasse (today's Axel-Springer-Strasse) was built from 1890 to 1891 from a design by the architecture office of **Cremer & Wolffenstein** and inaugurated on September 27, 1891. The redbrick neo-Romanesque building was built in the back courtyard and had seating for 1,800 worshipers. Inside, the individual ribs of the cross vault and main arcade above the Torah ark and prayer leader pulpit were colorfully painted. Services were conducted in the Liberal tradition with integrated organ music. A religion school, community apartments and various social institutions were housed in the front building. An inconspicuous-looking front building with a Jewish house of worship tucked away behind its protective walls became a model for other synagogue buildings in Berlin. The synagogue was demolished during the night of the November 1938 pogrom. Afterwards, it was used to store grain. The war-damaged building was torn down in 1956. Three plaques providing information on the synagogue hang in the driveway of the newly-built office building. An installation in the back courtyard created by Zvi Hecker, Micha Ullman and Eyal Weizman depicts stylized benches that indicate the original location of the synagogue pews.

SYNAGOGUE AT LÜTZOWSTRASSE 16 (TIERGARTEN) *

The synagogue on Lützowstrasse, modeled after the Lindenstrasse synagogue and designed by the same architects, **Cremer & Wolffenstein**, was built from 1897 to 1898 and inaugurated on September 11, 1898. The religion school, social institutions and a few business apartments were located in the front building. This synagogue was also hidden away in the back courtyard that was reached through a narrow gateway. A neo-Gothic redbrick building with about 1,900 seats was elevated over a cross-shaped floor plan. Liberal religious services were also conducted here with organ music. The synagogue was hardly damaged on the night of November 9, 1938: It was not set on fire for fear of damaging the neighboring buildings. Services were held here until Passover in April 1940. After suffering heavy damages from air raids, the ruins were torn down in 1954. A memorial plaque hangs on the building that has meanwhile been built on the synagogue property. It recalls the house of worship that once stood here.

ISRAELITE SYNAGOGUE COMMUNITY –
ADASS YISROEL

Tucholskystrasse 40 (Mitte), Tel. 281 31 35
Open: Monday–Thursday 9:30 am–5:30 pm, Friday 9:30 am–5:30 pm
Services: Friday 5 pm in winter and 6:30 pm in summer, Saturday
9:30 am

The 19th century saw the increasing liberalization of the official Jewish community with the New Synagogue becoming a center of Reform Judaism. But not all of the community's members wanted or
were able to go along with these developments. Consequently, the Orthodox Jewish Religious Society Adass Yisroel was founded in 1869.
After breaking away from the official Berlin Jewish community, the
Adass Yisroel congregation was officially recognized as an independent religious society on September 9, 1885. Its first Rabbi, **Esriel
Hildesheimer** (1820–1899), along with **Samson Raphael Hirsch**
(1808–1888), was one of the most important leaders of the neo-Or-
thodox movement in Germany. This movement tried to combine living in accordance with the *Halakhah*, the Jewish religious law, with an
openness for the culture and education of the surrounding non-Jewish world.

The community center of Adass Yisroel – with a synagogue, ritual
bathhouse (*Mikweh* in Hebrew), boys school, its own rabbinical seminary and a Talmud-Torah school was first located on Gipsstrasse. By
1873 it maintained its own cemetery on Wittlicher Strasse 2 (Weissensee) where the first burials took place in 1880.

In 1904 the new community center was dedicated in the former
Artilleriestrasse (today's Tucholskystrasse). The synagogue with 800
seats was situated in the second back courtyard and designed by **Johann Höniger** (1850–1913). It won an architecture award at the
time as the most beautiful sacred building in Germany. The synagogue survived the 1938 pogrom with minor damage, but was then
destroyed in World War II by aerial bombs. The ruins were torn down
in 1967. A Star of David survived the years of turmoil and can be seen
through the gateway above the portal of the first rear building.

In 1924, the Adass Yisroel congregation opened a second community center at Siegmunds Hof 11 (Tiergarten) that is today commemorated by a sculpture and memorial plaque. It also maintained the Israelite Hospital on Elsasserstrasse (today's Torstrasse). In December 1939 the Gestapo disbanded the congregation and forced its members to join the National Association of Jews in Germany.

On December 18, 1989 following long drawn out negotiations between the descendents of the congregation members and the GDR government, Adass Yisroel was re-established. After protracted disputes with the Berlin unitary congregation, Adass Yisroel was granted by the city administrative court the legal status as a Jewish congregation independent of the main community.

A new synagogue was inaugurated in the first rear courtyard building on Tucholskystrasse on *Purim* in 1990. Rabbi **Eliezer Ebner** has led the congregation since then. The community opened its own kosher restaurant, the Beth Café, in 1991, and it runs a kosher store named Kol Bo right around the corner at Auguststrasse 77/78. Today the community has 1,000 members.

SYNAGOGUE AT RYKESTRASSE 53
(PRENZLAUER BERG)

Tel. 448 52 98
Services: Friday 6 pm in winter, 7 pm in summer, Saturday 9:30 am

This very large synagogue on Rykestrasse is also located in a back courtyard that is reached by passing through two rounded arch gateways. It was also designed by the community's house architect **Johann Höniger**. The flat redbrick neo-Romanesque building was erected from 1903 to 1904. The ornately decorated triangular entrance gable and the building gable, which is softened by rounded arches, recall the medieval architecture of Brandenburg. The building was inaugurated on September 4, 1904.

The Rykestrasse synagogue has 2,000 seats. Its richly decorative main arch above the Torah ark is the only painted area of what is otherwise a rather simple interior. An organ and choir balcony was added for the religious services that were originally conducted in the

Reform tradition. Back then men and women did not sit apart as they do today. The synagogue survived the pogrom of 1938 relatively unscathed because it was located in a back courtyard. It was used by the Wehrmacht during the war.

After it was renovated in 1953 it was the only synagogue of the small Jewish community of East Berlin. The East German state rabbi, **Martin Riesenburger** (1896–1965), worked until his death in 1965 in the synagogue that he named "Temple of Peace." The largest synagogue in Germany is only filled on the High Holy Days. The wedding hall is used for the few visitors who attend the regular Conservative services.

In the fall of 1999, the **Ronald S. Lauder Foundation** school and offices moved into the front building where in the 1930s a religion and elementary school had once existed. This foundation, run by the son of Estée Lauder, the founder of the Estée Lauder cosmetic company, was established to support Jewish life in Central and Eastern Europe and to train teachers and educators in the Jewish traditions.

SYNAGOGUE AT MÜNCHENER STRASSE 37 (SCHÖNEBERG) *

In 1909, the year of its founding, the Schöneberg Synagogue Association purchased a plot of land to build a synagogue for the Orthodox Jews who lived there. The two-story domed building with Art Nouveau elements was erected in the back courtyard in the following year. There was space for more than 800 worshipers. A school and business apartments were housed in the front building. In the war-racked 1920s, the "*Ahavat Ahim* (in English: "brotherly love") Charity Organization of the Residents of the Schöneberg and Wilmersdorf Districts", which had been founded in 1917, set up a soup kitchen in the basement of the front building for the poor people in the neighborhood.

This synagogue was not destroyed during the November pogrom of 1938 because it was surrounded by residential buildings. The National Socialists were planning an anti-Jewish incitement exhibition. To this end they stole over 5,000 Torah scrolls and countless Jewish cultural objects that were temporarily stored in Jewish institutions.

A collection site was set up in the Münchener Strasse synagogue in 1941 for objects that Jews were no longer permitted to own. The front building was completely destroyed in World War II and the synagogue partly destroyed. On the grounds of the synagogue that was torn down in 1956 and where today a schoolyard exists, a cubist memorial stone commemorates the synagogue. Its rectangular stone blocks are interlocked like a prism and a seven-armed candelabra, the *Menorah*, and a inscription are carved out as a relief. The text on the ground plate in front of the memorial stone provides information on the synagogue. The memorial was created by Gerson Fehrenbach and dates back to 1963.

SYNAGOGUE AT FASANENSTRASSE * AND THE NEW JEWISH COMMUNITY CENTER

Fasanenstrasse 79/80 (Charlottenburg), Tel. 880 28-0
Open: Monday–Thursday 9 am–6 pm, Friday 9 am–3 pm

In the early 20th century, the Berlin Jewish community decided to build a new synagogue on Fasanenstrasse that – for the first time since the New Synagogue in the Oranienburger Strasse – was not inconspicuously tucked away in a back courtyard. In 1907 an architectural competition was held for the synagogue design and three first prizes were awarded. In the end the architect **Ehrenfried Hessel** received the commission. His design called for a massive rectangular structure with three domes. Kaiser Wilhelm II came to an official viewing a few days after the dedication on August 26, 1912. In the November pogrom of 1938 the synagogue was set ablaze and heavily damaged. The aerial bombs of the Second World War took care of the rest. The massive ruins were torn down in 1957–58.

A new **Jewish community center**, designed by **Dieter Knoblauch** and **Heinz Heise**, was built at the same site and inaugurated on September 27, 1959. Remains of the facade of the original old synagogue are arranged into the entrance portal of an otherwise rather sober-looking functional structure.

In addition to offices and a 600 seat hall that is also used as a prayer room, the center also houses the Jewish Adult Education Program and the kosher restaurant Gabriel's.

Since 1987 a stylized Torah scroll designed by the sculptor Richard Hess stands in front of the community center. In Hebrew and Latin lettering it admonishes with the biblical words: "There shall be one law for you and for the resident stranger among you."

SYNAGOGUE AT PESTALOZZISTRASSE 14 (CHARLOTTENBURG)

Tel. 313 84 11
Services: Friday 6 pm in winter, 7 pm in summer, Saturday 9:30 am

The synagogue on Pestalozzistrasse is situated in a back courtyard and was dedicated in 1912 as a private synagogue. The redbrick building designed by **Ernst Dorn** in neo-Romanesque style was intended to seat 1,400 worshipers of an Orthodox service. In 1919 the Jewish community took over the synagogue. It was set on fire in the pogrom night of 1938, but the blaze was put out by the fire department in order to prevent it from spreading to the neighboring buildings.

The first Jewish religious services after the war were held in this almost completely undamaged synagogue in summer 1945. The synagogue was inaugurated again in 1947 following its renovation. Today Liberal services are held here with organ and choir music, but the men and women sit apart. The prayers are almost continuously sung in Hebrew by the cantor and a mixed choir that sits on the balcony above the Torah ark. The well-known singer **Estrongo Nachama** was the long-standing head cantor there until his death in early 2000. The sermon, individual blessings and announcements are made in German. The prayer book that was printed especially for this synagogue and its liturgy provides the Hebrew text with a German translation on the adjacent page. The light and modestly decorated dome room is even well-filled during regular Sabbath services.

Bar Mitswah celebration in the synagogue on Pestalozzistrasse

Outside view of the synagogue on Pestalozzistrasse

SYNAGOGUE AT LEVETZOWSTRASSE 7/8 (TIERGARTEN) *

The community's house architect **Johann Höniger** designed a large neo-Classical synagogue with more than 2,000 seats. It was inaugurated in 1914 and also housed a religion school and community apartments. The entrance portal with a triangular gable decorated sparsely with a Star of David was supported by four Doric columns. The synagogue survived both the pogrom night of 1938 and World War II with light damages, but was torn down in 1955–56.

An elaborate memorial area designed by Peter Herbrich, Jürgen Wenzel and Theseus Bappert recalls the fact that the synagogue was misused as of 1941 as a collection site for Jews about to be deported. A railroad car symbolizes the deportation trains that departed from the Putlitzstrasse station. Plates engraved with pictures of Berlin synagogues have been placed on the ground.

SYNAGOGUE AT FRAENKELUFER 10 (KREUZBERG)

Tel. 614 51 31
Services: Friday 6 pm in winter, 7 pm in summer, Saturday 9:30 am

The synagogue, built by the community's house architect **Alexander Beer** (1873–1943) in neo-Classical style, was dedicated in 1916. The three-aisled basilica provided seats for 2,000 worshipers of Orthodox services. The impressive front facade contained four Doric columns, architrave and triangular gables. The synagogue was imbedded into a community center with community offices and residential areas, a weekday and youth synagogue.

The synagogue burned out during the pogrom night of 1938 and after 1942 was used by the Gestapo to store stolen Jewish property. War bombs destroyed the main synagogue and the ruins were torn down in 1958–59. All that remains today is the side wing where the weekday and youth synagogue used to be and where Conservative Sabbath services are held. A memorial plaque designed by Cornelia Lengfeld was hung in 1989 and added to in 1995.

SYNAGOGUE AT MARKGRAF-ALBRECHT-STRASSE 11/12 (WILMERSDORF) *

This Liberal synagogue, called the "Temple of Peace," was built in 1921. The prayer room seated 1,450 worshipers. The main congregation took over the private synagogue in 1928 after its expenses could no longer be covered. The synagogue was severely damaged by fire in the pogrom night of 1938 and the ruins were removed in 1959. A memorial plaque on the residential buildings that were built on the property after the war commemorates the synagogue.

SYNAGOGUE AT JOACHIMSTALER STRASSE 13 (CHARLOTTENBURG)

Tel. 884 20 30
Services: daily morning services (7:30 am or 8 am, Saturday 9:30 am) and evening services (half an hour before sunset, Friday after sunset)

This building originally belonged to the Jewish Lodge B'nai B'rith. As of 1933 it housed the Joseph Lehmann School of the Jewish Reform congregation and in 1939 also the VIII. Elementary School of the Jewish Community. After Berlin was divided, various community offices and Jewish organizations such as the Jewish National Fund and the Women's International Zionist Organization (WIZO) set up their offices here. Daily Orthodox services are now held in the largest hall, which was used by the lodge and as an auditorium and sports hall. Since the autumn of 2000 services are conducted in other rooms of the building according to the Sephardic tradition. A ritual bathhouse (*Mikweh* in Hebrew), was established in the basement. The building also houses other Jewish community administrative offices, the social affairs and religious administrations, offices of the Rabbi and the Jewish community youth center.

SYNAGOGUE AT PRINZREGENTENSTRASSE 69/70 (WILMERSDORF) *

The synagogue, inaugurated on September 16, 1930 was the last to be built in Berlin before the National Socialists came to power. **Alexander Beer**, the community's architect, designed the immense dome structure; he was murdered in the Theresienstadt concentration camp in 1943. The front building section facing the street housed a religion school, an elementary school and welfare agencies of the Jewish community. The house of worship had an organ and seating for 2,300 visitors of Liberal services. In the pogrom night of 1938 the synagogue was set ablaze and completely destroyed. It was not torn down until 1958. Today a residential house of the General Association of the Blind is located on the property. A memorial plaque commemorates the history of the synagogue.

SYNAGOGUE AT HERBARTSTRASSE 26 (CHARLOTTENBURG)

Tel. 321 20 56
Services: Friday 5:30 pm in winter, 6 pm in summer, Saturday 9:30 am

The small synagogue built in 1981 with only 135 seats belongs to the complex of the Jeanette Wolff Retirement Home and the Leo Baeck Home for the Elderly. The functional, plain building was designed by **Hans Wolff Grohmann**. Columns and religious objects from the former synagogue of the old age home on Iranische Strasse are thoughtfully integrated into the design. Conservative services are held here.

SYNAGOGUE AT HÜTTENWEG 46 (ZEHLENDORF)

Services: Friday 8:30 pm

The interior of the former synagogue of the US army was purchased by members of the Unity congregation in 1994 after the Americans left. The first services in the re-furnished synagogue were held on September 17, 1999 and led by head cantor **Estrongo Nachama**. Today the congregation has 120 members. Rabbi **Andreas Nachama** holds Liberal services here and once a week he offers a lesson in studying the scriptures. On September 17, 2004, exactly five years after its re-opening, the synagogue was officially recognized as a community institution and its rent paid by the community. Until then the status of the congregation had been an issue of debate. It was not until Albert Meyer, one of the co-initiators of the congregation, was elected community chairman, that the way was paved for its recognition.

Educational Institutions

TEACHING AND LEARNING IN JUDAISM

Learning in Judaism is a religious duty and scholars are highly respected in the community. Being able to read is one of the basic principles of religious life. In the traditional Jewish elementary school (*Heder* in Hebrew) boys learned to read at the early age of three. They learned the Hebrew alphabet first so that they could read the Torah. Afterwards, they could continue their education in the Talmud school (*Yeshivah* in Hebrew) where they studied rabbinical texts and medieval commentaries.

It is thanks to the Jewish Enlightenment that Jewish education has diversified. In Berlin, Moses Mendelssohn and his pupils pushed for the pioneering changes in Jewish education. The students of the newly established Jewish Free School were taught not only the Hebrew language and religious traditions; they also learned the German language and studied secular fields such as mathematics, geography and history. The first girls' schools were opened shortly thereafter.

In the 1930s the community maintained twenty-two general education schools and forty-nine religious schools. All Jewish educational institutions were forced to shut down on July 30, 1942. The last remaining pupils were deported with their teachers to the death camps.

The Jewish Adult Education Program was for many years after the war the only Jewish educational institution in Berlin. In the 1990s, with Russian immigration considerably enlarging the community, but also due to a stronger and more openly expressed Jewish self-confidence, the community began to open Jewish schools again.

Scholarly interest in Judaism as a subject in itself – like so many educational developments – had its origins in the Jewish Enlightenment. Leopold Zunz came up with the idea of a science of Judaism. He wanted to replace Jewish tradition with the scientific, historically-critical research of tradition. Enlightened Jews who regarded tradition of Jewish literature as a closed book should now scientifically study and systematize its sources and document its history. Initially, the science *of* Judaism was used to defend against anti-Jewish prejudices and hostilities and to serve the apologetic self-presentation of Judaism. But it increasingly developed into a science *from* Judaism that non-Jewish scholars could also engage in.

In the early 20th century the science of Judaism is referred to as Jewish studies. It has developed into a multi-disciplinary field that uses philosophical, historical, religious and sociological methods to investigate all manifestations of Judaism.

Characteristic of the anti-Jewish tendencies of academia at this time is the refusal of German educational authorities to accept Jewish studies as a subject in its own right at the German university. The scholarly investigation of Judaism in an academic environment was only possible at theological institutions, but they tended to be heavily missionary and even antisemitic. Otherwise, Jewish studies was only taught at private institutions such as the College for the Science of Judaism in Berlin and the Jewish Theological Seminary in Breslau.

Only after the Shoah, when all the Jewish scholars from Germany had been forced into exile or murdered, did (West) German universities begin to establish academic chairs in Jewish studies. The first institute for Jewish studies in Germany was founded at the Freie Universität in Berlin in 1964. The Center for Antisemitism Research was established at the Berlin Technical University in 1982.

JEWISH ELEMENTARY AND SECONDARY SCHOOL, COLLEGE PREPARATORY HIGH SCHOOL – THE FORMER JEWISH FREE SCHOOL

Grosse Hamburger Strasse 27 (Mitte)

Engraved in stone over the entrance portal reads the German inscription "Jewish Community Boys' School."

As early as July 13, 1761, Veitel Heine Ephraim and Daniel Itzig, both influential bankers, signed a petition to the Prussian state asking permission to found a school. In 1778 the time had come. On the initiative of **Moses Mendelssohn**, the Jewish Free School was founded by **David Friedländer** (1750–1834), **Isaak Daniel Itzig** (1750–1806) and **Naphtali Herz Wessely** (1725–1805).

It was the first school in Germany to combine religious instruction with a secular education. Most of the seventy to eighty Jewish and Christian pupils came from poor homes. After completing their studies, many of the Jewish pupils became teachers in the East Prussian provinces, where they often spread the idea of Jewish Enlightenment and worked for the emancipation of Jews. In 1819 the school commission passed the Karlsbad Resolutions which forbid Jewish and Christian pupils from being taught jointly by Jewish and Christian teachers. In 1826 the private school was taken over by the Jewish community.

After moving a number of times the school finally settled permanently at the property on Grosse Hamburger Strasse in 1863. The present building was built in 1905–06 and inaugurated on November 26, 1906. It was designed by the Jewish community's house architect **Johann Höniger**, who also planned the synagogue of Adass Yisroel and the synagogues on Ryke and Levetzowstrasse. A teacher's college (1859–1925) and in 1919 the Hebrew College were also located in the building. The bust of Moses Mendelssohn was placed in the front garden in 1909 and destroyed by SA men in 1941. The boys' and girls' schools were combined in 1931.

The political situation worsened when the Nazis assumed power and this was reflected by the rising number of Jewish pupils attending the school: In 1932–33, 470 school children were counted; by 1934 the number had already risen to 1,025. On June 30, 1942 the school was closed by the German authorities along with all the other Jewish educational institutions. Afterwards, the home for the elderly next door was evacuated and misused as a collection site. The residents of the home were lodged in the former school until their deportation. **Martin Riesenburger** held religious services in the assembly hall where concerts and plays were also performed.

After standing empty for years, the building was used as a vocational school for industry salesmen. In 1983, for the 250th birthday of Friedrich Nicolai, the journalist Heinz Knobloch arranged to have a plaque designed by Gerhard Thieme hung on the building front with a relief of

Moses Mendelssohn and his life motto: "Search for truth, love beauty, desire good, and do the best."

After German reunification, the Jewish community's request to have the building returned was granted. Since August 1992 the building has been used by the Jewish community as an elementary school. A year later, on August 6, 1993, a Jewish secondary school and college preparatory high school were founded. Hebrew is offered as a third foreign language to ninth graders and up. The schoolchildren are also taught the basics of Jewish religion and history. The private all-day school is also attended by non-Jews, most of whom come from Christian and academic families. Like all the Jewish institutions in Berlin, major security measures have been installed to protect it from an attack by rightwing extremists.

FORMER COLLEGE FOR THE SCIENCE OF JUDAISM

Tucholskystrasse 9 (formerly Artilleriestrasse 14; Mitte)

On January 5, 1870 **Moritz Lazarus** (1824–1903) and **Salomon Neumann** (1819–1908) founded the curatorship for the College for the Science of Judaism in Berlin (Hochschule für die Wissenschaft des Judentums). Classes began on May 6, 1872. The college had a number of different locations, but on October 22, 1907 it moved into its own new building on Artilleriestrasse 14 (today's Tucholskystrasse) that was designed by the Jewish community's house architect **Johann Höniger**. The Prussian school authority demanded in 1883 that it cease to call itself a college. Its original name was not re-approved until 1920 in the Weimar Republic, but by 1934 it was again banned by the National Socialists.

The college was open to all students regardless of their religious affiliation or gender. It trained rabbis, preachers and religious teachers. Lectures and seminars on the entire spectrum of Jewish literature and history were offered. The students had to simultaneously be enrolled in a faculty of the Berlin University. Excellent teachers and famous scholars such as **Abraham Geiger**, **David Cassel**, **Julius Guttmann**, **Ismar Elbogen** and **Leo Baeck** taught at this school. Beginning in 1919,

Baeck taught the history of religion, Jewish studies and the theory of education. He was also the school's last rector.

Regina Jonas, the first German female rabbi, studied here from 1924 to 1930. In her final examination she addressed the question: "Can a women serve as a rabbi?" and proved how religious law allows for the ordination of women. Nonetheless, until 1935 when she was ordained as a rabbi, she was only able to work as a religion teacher. She held sermons in various Liberal synagogues in Berlin and showed herself to have a special talent in providing spiritual comfort to the distressed Jewish community members. After doing forced labor in a cardboard packaging factory in Berlin-Lichtenberg, she was deported with her mother to Theresienstadt on November 6, 1942. On October 12, 1944 Regina Jonas was sent to the Auschwitz concentration camp where she was murdered. In June 2001 a memorial plaque was hung at her last residence, Krausnickstrasse 6 (Mitte).

The college reached its pinnacle in 1932 with 155 enrolled students. The library had 60,000 books and an important collection of Jewish ritual objects. Its entire holdings were lost after the school was shut down by the Nation Socialists on July 19, 1942.

In April 1999 the building was returned to the Jewish community, restored and re-opened under the new name **Leo Baeck House**. It now houses the headquarters of the Central Council of Jews in Germany that used to be located in Frankfurt am Main. The lion's head over the portal of the former College for the Science of Judaism survived the tumultuous history of the building and symbolizes in Judaism the strength of wisdom.

FORMER ORTHODOX RABBINICAL SEMINARY

Tucholskystrasse 40 (formerly Artilleriestrasse 31; Mitte)

The Rabbinical Seminary for Orthodox Judaism in Berlin (Rabbiner-Seminar für das orthodoxe Judenthum zu Berlin) was founded on October 22, 1873 as conscious reaction to the College for the Science of Judaism. The academic program took six years to complete and ended with a comprehensive final exam. As was the case with the College for the Science of Judaism, the students had to be simultaneously enrolled at the Berlin university in order to take scholarly courses.

The orthodox rabbinical seminary quickly established itself as the most important school for orthodox rabbis in all of Europe. In its first year it had only twenty students, but by the 1890s, when it had reached the pinnacle of its success, sixty-seven students were enrolled at the school.

The educational institution was first located at Gipsstrasse 12a. After the new community center of Adass Yisroel relocated to Artilleriestrasse 31 (today's Tucholskystrasse 40) in 1904, the rabbinical seminary moved into the front building. In 1934, **Meir Hildesheimer**, the head rabbi at the time, tried in vain to move the seminary to Palestine. The rabbinical seminary was forced to close on November 10, 1938.

FORMER JEWISH GIRLS' SCHOOL

Auguststrasse 11–13 (Mitte)

The first girls' school of the Jewish community was founded in 1835. The redbrick building on Auguststrasse was built in 1927–28 based on plans by the community's house architect **Alexander Beer** in the sober style of "Neue Sachlichkeit." A 200 square meter roof garden served as a recess area. The girls' school opened here on August 31, 1930. In 1932, 441 girls were taught here; by 1937 the number had risen to 869. The increase in the number of pupils had to do with the growing discrimination against Jewish children in public schools.

This girls' elementary school was also forced to close on June 30, 1942. The building was used as a military hospital during World War II. In East Germany and after its collapse, a secondary school existed here until 1995–96. The building was desperately in need of repair when it was returned to the Berlin Jewish community, but there are currently no funds available for this.

JEWISH ADULT EDUCATION PROGRAM

Office: Fasanenstrasse 79/80 (Charlottenburg), Tel. 880 28-263
Office hours: Monday–Thursday 9 am–3 pm
Classrooms: Oranienburger Strasse 29 (Mitte)

The Jewish Adult Education Program founded in 1962 was originally located at the community center on Fasanenstrasse. Since German re-unification, only the offices remain there; the classrooms are now located at Oranienburger Strasse.

The Adult Education Program is geared toward Jewish and non-Jewish adults who are interested in learning about Jewish culture and education. Its yearly trimester program offers Hebrew and Yiddish language courses, seminars on Jewish history, religious instruction, courses on philosophy, art and literature. The curriculum is augmented by lectures, readings, podium discussions and concerts. Since 1995, it organizes a Jewish film festival together with the "Friends of the German Cinema." The current course program is available at the community center and can be mailed out upon request.

HEINZ GALINSKI SCHOOL

Waldschulallee 73 (Charlottenburg), Tel. 301 19 40

The elementary school named after the longtime chairman of the Berlin Jewish community was dedicated on September 15, 1995. The modern design was created by the Israeli architect **Zvi Hecker**. The outline of the six connected buildings arranged around an inner courtyard is styled after a sunflower. The ground plan of the building ensemble is set into the wall of exposed concrete at the entrance and serves as the school insignia. The sharply angled intersection of walls, the different colored protruding blind arches and the rounded segments lend the building a strong dynamic. About 250 Jewish and non-Jewish pupils attend this school.

Jewish School on Grosse Hamburger Strasse

Heinz Galinski School

Social Institutions

JEWISH CHARITY

The universal command to love one's neighbor serves in Judaism as a call for a social commitment to the needy. The "acts of love" entail taking care of the ill, the elderly, orphans and widows, educating poor children, burying the dead, providing comfort, making peace, helping strangers and giving to charity.

An extremely diverse Jewish charity work developed from this all-encompassing duty, financed completely through private donations and run to a large degree through volunteer work. Countless social services were founded including homes for the elderly, hospitals, orphanages, children's and refugee homes, homes for the blind and soup kitchens.

The first charitable foundation of this kind, called *Hekdesh* (in English: "consecrated"), was founded in 1703. It established the hospital at Oranienburger Strasse 8 in the mid-18th century. When the Jewish community limited its assistance to the needy who maintained the orthodox way of life, Joseph Mendelssohn founded the Society of Friends with other like-minded followers of the Enlightenment in 1792. It worked for the mutual support of the poor and ill and sought a dialogue between Jews and Christians. It existed until 1938 when the National Socialists forced it to close.

Modeled after lodges in the United States, the first Jewish lodge, the German National Lodge B'nai B'rith was founded in 1882. This male order was involved in cultural activities, but more importantly engaged in social work for the poor, sick, jobless and victims of persecution. Women, who were excluded from the lodge work in Germany, organized their own sister associations.

The Central Welfare Office of German Jews was founded in Germany in 1917 and served as an umbrella organization for over 200 Jewish aid organizations. It was reestablished after the war in 1951 at its original location, Oranienburger Strasse 31 in Berlin. In the late 1920s, the *Jewish Yearbook for Greater Berlin* listed twelve Jewish orphanages and children's homes as well as eight Jewish homes for the elderly in the German capital.

During National Socialism the financial situation for Jewish citizens worsened with each new decree. In October 1935 the Jewish Winter Aid was founded. It organized the distribution of food, clothes and coal. In 1933 the Central Office for Jewish Economic Aid was founded to provide legal advice, credit, jobs and retraining for Jewish owners of small businesses and self-employed Jews. It was closed down in 1940.

FORMER HOME FOR THE ELDERLY AT GROSSE HAMBURGER STRASSE 26 (MITTE) *

The first Jewish home for the elderly was founded on July 27, 1827 at Oranienburger Strasse 6–8. Later, on July 28, 1844 it moved into a new building at Grosse Hamburger Strasse 26. The residents lived in single and double rooms and could use the library and a number of other residential rooms. The sanitary facilities and kitchen were repeatedly modernized to keep up with current standards. **Martin Riesenburger**, who later became the state rabbi of the East German Jewish communities, began work in this old-age home in 1933.

In 1942 the Gestapo evacuated the home and misused it as a collection site. Prison cells with barred windows were set up on the first floor and in the basement. Armed guards kept watch over the building, which was secured with spotlights on the back and front facade. Despite these measures, a few inmates were able to escape across the cemetery during a bomb explosion on New Years' Eve of 1943.

Towards the end of the war the building was destroyed by bombs and later torn down. A memorial stone and plaque recall the deportation of Berlin Jews. A sculpture group designed by Will Lammert was erected to the right of the stone.

FORMER HOME FOR THE ELDERLY AT SCHÖNHAUSER ALLEE 22 (PRENZLAUER BERG)

Bertha and **Moritz Manheimer** financed the new old-age home on the occasion of their silver anniversary in 1880. Moritz Manheimer had run a women's clothing company with his brother Valentin but in 1872 he began dedicating all his time to his many charitable foundations. The Manheimers are buried at the Jewish cemetery on Schönhauser Allee, right behind the home for the elderly.

The redbrick building was dedicated on November 11, 1883 and offered a home to eighty-nine needy elderly people. In 1941 the remaining residents were deported to Auschwitz along with the institute's staff. The building was later used by the SS. After the war a police station was set up here. The presently empty building was returned to the Jewish community and is in urgent need of renovation.

LEO BAECK HOME FOR THE ELDERLY

Herbartstrasse 26 (Charlottenburg)

JEANETTE WOLFF HOME – JEWISH SENIOR CITIZENS CENTER

Dernburgerstrasse 36 (Charlottenburg)

The two institutions for Jewish senior citizens are located in the same building complex. The rabbi and scholar Leo Baeck was the last president of the National Representation of German Jews; the social democrat politician Jeanette Wolff was a member of the German Parliament and Berlin House of Representatives.

Both residences were dedicated in 1981. Dining room, cafeteria, hairdresser, library and even a small synagogue are available to the residents who reside in the 140 residential apartments.

FORMER COMMUNITY CENTER AT AUGUSTSTRASSE 17 (MITTE)

Over the course of its history, the building at Auguststrasse 17 housed a number of Jewish social institutions. First, in 1895, a nurses' hostel for the neighboring Jewish hospital was established here. From 1917 to 1920 the Jewish Peoples Association managed a number of homes for Jewish refugees from Russia. In 1920 the Association of Eastern European Jews and the Workers' Welfare Office of Jewish Organizations in Germany used the building.

The latter organization looked after Jewish refugees, offering legal advice and helping them to find living accommodations and work. In 1929 alone, 11,543 Jews were registered here as unemployed. As of 1933 a hostel for homeless women and girls and the Welfare Office of the Mitte district, both institutions of the Jewish community, were also located here.

FORMER JEWISH HOSPITAL AND COMMUNITY CENTER AT AUGUSTSTRASSE 14–16 (MITTE)

After the building on Oranienburger Strasse no longer met the needs of the Jewish Hospital, it moved to a new building in the back courtyard of Auguststrasse in 1861. The severe-looking brick building was designed by **Eduard Knoblauch**, who also built the New Synagogue on Oranienburger Strasse shortly thereafter. Both institutions were situated on the same long stretched out piece of property belonging to the Jewish community. The hospital was initially equipped with 120 beds and a modern sanitary facility with bathing rooms and water closets.

After the hospital moved to Exerzierstrasse in the Wedding district in 1914, a number of social and cultural institutions of the Jewish community were set up here. The Jewish Yearbook of 1928 mentions the following institutions located in the building complex at Auguststrasse 14–16: The Girls' Hostel of the Berlin Branch of the Federation of Jewish Women, Nursery for Infants, Greater Berlin *Hevrah Kaddisha* Burial Society, Jewish Community Cookery School, *Ahavah* Jewish Children's Home, Sewing Room for Women and Girls, Dental Clinic and Orthopedic Gymnasium of the Jewish Children's Aid Agency, Nursery of the Jewish Community Welfare Office, *Ahavah* Jewish Girls' Hostel, *Agudas Yisroel* Kindergarten and the *Peah* Clothing Stores of the Jewish community.

The Jewish community's home for Eastern European refugee children has been called *Ahavah* (in English: "love") since 1922. In 1934–1935, some of the children were able to emigrate to Palestine with the director. From 1941 to 1943 the Gestapo used the building as a collection site for old and sickly Jews.

After the war a special school, secondary school and boarding school for children with poor eyesight were established here. After German reunification, this extremely dilapidated building complex was returned to the Jewish community, which will probably use it for the community's administration offices.

FORMER ISRAELITE HOSPITAL

Torstrasse 146 (formerly Elsässer Strasse 85; Mitte)

From 1909 onward, the Israelite Hospital, which was founded by Adass Yisroel nine years earlier and until then had been housed in other unsuitable locations, moved into this four-story brick building. The founding of a hospital of the independent orthodox congregation was made possible by a generous financial donation from **Abraham Zamory**, a textile manufacturer and co-founder of the congregation. The hospital provided medical treatment to all patients, regardless of their social class, gender, or origins and it served kosher food. In late September 1941 the hospital was forced to shut down.

The building was then used both as a hostel for the Hitler youth and as an office of the National Association of Jews in Germany. In the postwar era the building first housed a Berlin police precinct and later an office of the German railroad company.

In May of 2002 the building, which has stood empty since German reunification, was vandalized and a number of objects belonging to the community were destroyed. A plaque indicating the historical significance of this highly dilapidated building has yet to be erected here.

JEWISH HOSPITAL AND HERMANN-STRAUSS-HOSPITAL

Iranische Strasse 2–4 (formerly Exerzierstrasse 11a; Wedding)

In 1914 the Jewish Hospital moved to its new location at Exerzierstrasse 11a (today's Iranische Strasse 2–4) in Wedding. Seven new buildings with 270 beds were built on the property belonging to the Jewish community. Since 1902 a Jewish home for the elderly was situated right across the street at Exerzierstrasse 13 (today's Iranische Strasse 3).

In 1941 the SS established a collection site and prison in the pathology station of the hospital. The inmates were deported from here to the Theresienstadt concentration camp or to the Auschwitz death camp. Half the hospital staff was deported on March 10, 1943 in what is known as the "Hospital Action." After the National Association of Jews in Germany and the Jewish Cultural Union of Berlin were disbanded by the Gestapo on June 10, 1943, there were only two Jewish institutions left in Berlin: the Jewish Cemetery in Weissensee and the Jewish Hospital on Exerzierstrasse. But both institutions were kept under strict surveillance by the Gestapo. The hospital's head doctor, Dr. **Walter Lustig** (1891–1945), who lived in a so-called "mixed marriage with an Aryan woman" was given the responsibility of directing the hospital and selecting the last Jews in Berlin for deportation. He apparently fulfilled his duties diligently and with absolute compliance. After the war he was charged with collaboration and believed to have been executed by the Soviet Military Administration.

Hidden Jews and Jews living with false identity papers who were denounced and discovered were brought to the Gestapo prison in the hospital. Torture was used to force them to betray other "illegal" Jews. Jews from all over Germany who had been able to survive in "mixed marriages" but then labeled no longer fit for work were deported by the Gestapo to Iranische Strasse in Berlin. Up to one thousand Jews were interned in the hospital under inhuman conditions until the end of the war. Many of them could not be deported because of their poor health. The last death transport departed from the hospital on March 27, 1945.

In May of 1945 eight hundred survivors, most of them severely ill and under-nourished, were liberated in the hospital. Even before they were fully recuperated, some of them began to revive the Jewish community. But most of them left Germany as soon as they could.

Since the hospital was now too large and expensive for what had become a relatively small Jewish community, it was converted in 1963 into a public hospital under the sponsorship of a foundation. In accordance with its statute, five representatives of the Jewish community sit on the board to ensure a continued close contact between the two institutions. Only recently, with the rapid growth of the Jewish community, are an increasing number of Jewish patients again being treated there. A small synagogue that was used after the war as a changing room for a bathing facility, has been renovated and was consecrated with a religious service at the end of December 2000. The affiliated Jewish nursing home is named after **Hermann Strauss** (1868–1944), the last director of the Jewish Hospital, who died in the Theresienstadt concentration camp.

FORMER JEWISH ORPHANAGE

Berliner Strasse 120/121 (Pankow)

As early as 1882 an orphanage founded by **Hermann Makower** was located here. In 1912 a new building was erected for the Jewish orphanage, which opened a year later. The three-story neo-Baroque building could accommodate up to one hundred children. The artfully painted coffered ceiling of the synagogue in the building was donated by Josef Garbáty, the owner of the cigarette factory next door. After the orphanage was forcibly closed and the last children were deported, the Reich Security Main Office set up offices here. After the war the building first housed the Pankow district administration and

German Sport Association, later the Polish embassy and since 1970 the Cuban embassy. The Walter and Margarete Cajewitz Foundation bought the building from the Jewish Claims Conference in 1999 and the city library, the nursing school of the "Diakonisches Werk," and an addiction assistance center moved in. The hall of prayer was re-opened in early 2002 after the precious ceiling was restored. Concerts, readings and exhibitions, most of them of an intercultural nature, take place here irregularly.

Jewish Cemeteries

FUNERAL RITES

Jewish cemeteries are laid out for eternity; the gravesites remain preserved, they are not dismantled or reused. Translated, the usual Hebrew expressions for a cemetery are: the "House of Graves," the "House of Life," or the "Eternal House."

As a rule, burial is carried out as soon as possible after death. Cremation is not practiced in traditional Judaism, for there is a firm belief in the resurrection of the dead. As a sign of their mourning and grief, the closest relatives of the deceased tear at their clothes. Today, only a piece of clothing is torn symbolically, for example a necktie or an attached piece of ribbon. Traditionally, the eldest son says an Aramaic prayer at the graveside, the *Kaddish*. This prayer does not lend expression to the grief of the bereaved, but solely praises God.

Visitors place stones in commemoration on the gravestone instead of flowers. Any kind of cult of the dead is undesired. Everyone is equal in death; social and intellectual differences are abolished. The dead, wrapped in a plain cloth, are buried in simple wooden coffins. But the adoption of non-Jewish customs from the majority culture has led to extensive differentiation. There are numerous elaborately decorated gravesites in the Schönhauser Allee cemetery and even more so at the cemetery of the main community in Weissensee, which was established later. The deceased's individuality and naturally their family's financial resources increasingly determined the size and artistic realization of the grave.

The Hebrew inscriptions frequently follow set formulations, many of which are abbreviated. The inscription almost always begins with two Hebrew letters (*Peh* and *Tet* or *Nun*), which are abbreviations for the introductory words (in English: "here lies or [is] buried"). The order of the Hebrew letters at the end of the inscription (*Taw*, *Nun*, *Tsadeh*, *Bet and Heh*) is the abbreviation of a Hebrew eulogy, which in English translation reads: "May his/her soul be taken into the bond of (eternal) life." As assimilation increased, Hebrew was used less and less for grave inscriptions, giving way to German. Gravestones are often inscribed with both languages.

If pictorial representations are to be found on Jewish gravestones, then these are almost exclusively Jewish symbols. They are often Stars of David, but there are also depictions of menorahs, crowns, grapes and animals. The animal depictions allude mainly to the name of the deceased. For scholars we also find lions, covenant tablets or Torah scrolls. Hands splayed out offering a blessing are reserved for the descendants of priests (*Kohen* in Hebrew), who are recognizable by their name, for example, Cohen, Kahn or Katz. The motif of the pitcher – to be seen occasionally together with a basin – refers to the descendants of the Levites, who were once the temple servants.

At the same time though, adaptation to non-Jewish surroundings has meant that some symbols from originally non-Jewish sources have found their way into Jewish cemeteries. Branches, wreaths, garlands, torches, hourglasses, fallen trees or roses are especially common in the cemetery of the main community in Weissensee. The sculptural depictions of damaged pillars, tree stumps, vases and trophies are also part of this development. Flower bouquets and decorative flowerbeds were also unknown in Jewish tradition.

Every male visitor to a Jewish cemetery has to wear some form of head covering. If need be, a simple paper cap can be borrowed at the entrance. The former burial fraternities (*Hevrah kaddisha*), which provided services on an honorary basis, were entrusted with a number of tasks, including the nursing of the terminally ill, the ritual washing of the body, the guarding of the body to prevent any possible instance of its violation and soiling, wrapping the body in the burial shroud, the burial of the dead and, finally, accompanying the bereaved family through all the funeral formalities. Today, modern funeral companies take care of these tasks.

JUDEN-KIEWER (SPANDAU) *

To view the gravestones: Zitadelle Spandau, Am Juliusturm,
Tel. 334 62 70

The expression "Kiewer," which in this spelling is verified in older chronicles, comes from the Hebrew word *Kewer* (in English: "grave"). It is estimated that around 150 to 200 Jews lived in Spandau in the 13th and early 14th centuries. The oldest gravestone found here bears the date 1244. Jews from Berlin were also buried in Spandau, which may indicate that they did not have their own cemetery at this time. After the Jews were expelled from Berlin and Brandenburg in 1510, the Christian inhabitants destroyed the cemetery and used the gravestones as building material for the citadel that was built in the following years.

In 1955–56, nineteen Jewish gravestones masoned into the wall were found during reconstruction work on the foundations of the Spandau citadel. Following further excavations in the 1980s, a total of sixty-six gravestones and smaller fragments have been discovered by now. These gravestones are mostly boulders that were hardly worked, adorned solely with short, plain Hebrew inscriptions. Most of the gravestones are from the first half of the 14th century.

Fifty-seven gravestones can be viewed in the casemates of the Spandau citadel, however only after making arrangements per telephone. Another four gravestones from the Spandau Kiewer are located on both sides of the main path at the Jewish cemetery on Heerstrasse.

CEMETERY AT GROSSE HAMBURGER STRASSE 26 (MITTE)

Right in the middle of the Spandauer Vorstadt is a small green oasis on Grosse Hamburger Strasse. This harmless looking green space covers the oldest cemetery of Berlin's modern Jewish community, destroyed however in the period of National Socialism. This cemetery was officially opened in 1672 and had to be closed for capacity reasons in 1827.

This small cemetery is supposed to have once held more than 12,000 graves. In 1872, the former cemetery administrator Leiser Landshuth compiled a handwritten register of 2,767 decipherable gravestones with their inscriptions. All of the inscriptions were in Hebrew script, even the few that expressed German phrases.

The Gestapo almost completely destroyed the cemetery in 1943: they had Jewish forced laborers dig a slit trench across the cemetery grounds and shore it up with gravestones.

Numerous famous members of the first founding generation of the Jewish community were buried in the cemetery, including the rabbi David Fränkel (1707–1762), the court jeweler and mint lessee Veitel Heine Ephraim (1703–1775), the philosopher Moses Mendelssohn (1729–1786), and the doctor Marcus Herz (1747–1803).

Today only a single freestanding gravestone can be found on the cemetery on Grosse Hamburger Strasse. It is the grave of **Moses Mendelssohn**. Born in Dessau to a poor Torah scribe and deformed by an atrophied spinal column all his life, Mendelssohn walked to Berlin as a fourteen year old in 1743, following his teacher David Fränkel, who was the senior rabbi of Berlin from 1743 to 1762. In years of private study Moses Mendelssohn first learnt German, French, English, Latin and Greek, before studying philosophy and mathematics. Beginning in 1754, he enjoyed a deep friendship with Gotthold Ephraim Lessing (1729–1781), who then set a monument to Mendelssohn with the title figure of his drama *Nathan the Wise*. Mendelssohn's translations into German included the five books of Moses and the Psalms. His principal religious-philosophical work, *Jerusalem, or Religious Power and Judaism*, was published in 1783. On a journey to Hamburg Moses Mendelssohn met Fromet Gugenheim (1737–1812), whom he was finally able to marry in 1762. Fame was achieved above all by their grandson, the conductor and composer Felix Mendelssohn Bartholdy (1809–1847). Since he was baptized, like almost all Mendelssohn descendants, his grave is located in the cemetery of the Jerusalem and New Church Parish at Mehringdamm 21 in Kreuzberg.

In 1880, as a sign of esteem, the original gravestone of Moses Mendelssohn was replaced by a new, larger granite stone with base and triangular pediment, which was then destroyed in the aforementioned Gestapo action of 1943. The third gravestone for Mendelssohn, this time of seashell limestone in a very plain, square-shaped design, was erected in 1962 roughly where the former grave was believed to have been. Due to weather erosion it was then replaced by a fourth in 1990, the one still to be seen today. In translation the Hebrew inscription, which does not entirely correspond to the German, reads (additions for making the text more readable are given in brackets):

"Here lies the sage Rabbi Moses from Dessau. He was born on the twelfth (day of the month) Elul (of the year) 5489. He passed away on the fourth day (of the week = Wednesday), the fifth (day of the month) Shevat. And he was buried on the next morning, on the fifth day (= Thursday), the sixth (day) of the same (month Shevat of the year) 5546. May his soul be taken into the bond of life."

The use of the Hebrew names of the month, the Hebrew calendar, and abbreviated introductory and concluding phrases are typical. Remarkable in contrast are the honorable titles of "sage" and "rabbi," which are missing in the German version.

The cemetery was classified as a historical park and placed under heritage protection in 1974. As early as 1948, the board of the Berlin Jewish community fixed a bilingual commemorative plaque on the southern wall reminding visitors of the cemetery's history. The attentive visitor can still discover destroyed sarcophagus graves, imprints of vaults in the wall and base remains along the landscaped sides of the cemetery.

Set in the southern wall of the cemetery and thus protected from the devastation, nineteen gravestones, some greatly weathered, have been preserved. They were removed in 1988 for restoration. Today they are kept at the Jewish cemetery of the main community in Weissensee. A multilingual, illustrated information panel was erected in 2001.

CEMETERY AT SCHÖNHAUSER ALLEE 23-25 (PRENZLAUER BERG)

Open: Monday–Thursday 8 am–4 pm, Friday 8 am–1 pm

The cemetery in the Schönhauser Allee officially opened in 1827. Until its closure in 1880 a total of 22,500 individual graves and 750 family graves were laid. During the Second World War the mortuary and adjacent smaller buildings as well as numerous gravestones, particularly in field J, were destroyed by bombs and shells. A commemorative stone located at the former site of the mortuary, directly to the left of the cemetery entrance, recalls these events. It bears the inscription: "Here you stand silently. But do not remain silent when you turn around." A new building was erected here that is to be officially opened at the end of 2005 and in which a lapidary with an exhibition of gravestones and information on Jewish burial culture is to be housed. Today the cemetery is listed as a historical monument.

Whoever has one to two hours at their disposal, the following tour that passes the graves of a few selected renowned persons and particularly remarkable graves is recommended. The route begins at the entrance, turns left onto the path between fields L1 and L4, then turns back again, passing the honor row, and follows the cemetery wall in a clockwise direction back to the entrance.

Following the path for approximately thirty-five meters we reach, on the left-hand side (field L4) behind the black granite memorial of the Croner family, the grave of **Gerson von Bleichröder** (1822–1893). The gravestone, designed by Reinhold Begas, is of Carrara marble. Nobility coats-of-arms adorn the square base. The freestanding gravestone is crowned with a large, decorated vase. The inscription comes from the Biblical prophet Isaiah and reads: "He was a man, as a hiding place from the wind, and a covert from the tempest; as rivers of water in a dry place, as the shadow of a great rock in a weary land." In 1859 Gerson von Bleichröder became the personal financial advisor and confidant of Otto von Bismarck and court banker to Wilhelm I. He financed Prussia's war against Austria in 1866 and after the Franco-

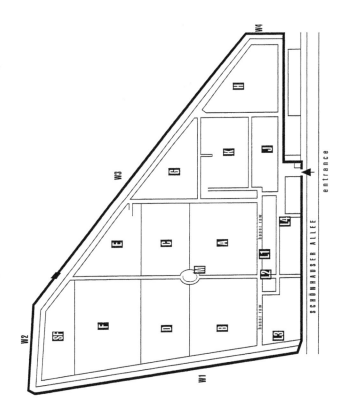

Prussian War of 1870–71 assumed responsibility for French reparation payments to Germany. In recognition of his services he became the first non-baptized Jew to be elevated to the hereditary peerage in Prussia in 1872. Bleichröder was a member of the representative assembly and, at different times, also of the board of the Jewish community.

At the next intersection on the left we find on field L3 the family grave of the entrepreneur and patron **James Henry Simon** (1851–1932). It is made up of three plain stones of black granite. As a partner in a cotton company, which soon developed into one of the world's largest textile enterprises, Simon became one of the richest men in Prussia. He was a driving force behind the founding of the German Orient Society in 1896 and financed excavations in Jericho, Babylon and Tell el-Amarna. Later he donated the valuable finds, which included the world-famous Nofretete bust, to the Near East and Egyptian Museum. Simon was not only well-known as a patron of the arts, but was also active in charities. His company went bankrupt in 1927 during the worldwide economic crisis and Simon lost almost his entire fortune.

Turning back along the same path we reach another path, opposite the memorial, that leads into the cemetery for a short stretch between fields L and J. At the next fork, the left path takes us between fields A and L. Here begins the cemetery's honor row, which was laid out on the western side of fields A and B, now to our right. The tall and often severely weathered gravestones are of very similar shape and plain, unadorned design.

Located roughly in the middle of the honor row on field A is the grave of **Michael Sachs** (1808–1864). The rabbi was born in Glogau, Silesia. After preaching in Prague for ten years, he came to Berlin in 1844, where he served as a rabbi until his death. He was regarded as a brilliant and popular preacher. Although he vehemently opposed introducing the organ to the synagogue service, he nevertheless supported the reform movement by translating prayer books into German. Educated in philosophy, Middle Eastern studies and classical philology, he was an important scholar and member of the association advocating the Science of Judaism. Together with its founder Leopold Zunz, he translated the Hebrew Bible into German.

Ironically, a lifelong opponent of Sachs is buried only a little further on, the radical reformer and rabbi of the temple in the Johannisstrasse, **Samuel Holdheim** (1806–1860). When Holdheim died, Sachs threatened to resign if the deceased was buried in the honor row. But he was buried here – and Sachs remained in office nonetheless. Born in Kempno near Posen, Holdheim received a traditional education in the Torah and Talmud. After a failed marriage to an educated women who taught him German and secular subjects, he studied philosophy in Prague. Already during his time as rabbi in Frankfurt/Oder he preached in German and demanded a reform of the traditional Jewish educational system. As the province rabbi for Mecklenburg-Schwerin he undertook a phased reform of the religious services and founded a school based on his ideas. He came to Berlin in 1847 to work as a rabbi in the newly founded reform community. Here he introduced radical innovations, for example moving the service to Sunday, abandoning the prescribed head cover for men in the synagogue and circumcision.

Next to Holdheim's grave are the two gravestones of the couple **Emma** (1816–1878) and **Baruch Auerbach** (1793–1864). Baruch Auerbach was director of the community's school for boys for twenty-two years. In 1833 he founded the "Baruch Auerbach Orphan and Education Institutes for Jewish Boys and Girls." Not a wealthy man himself, Auerbach financed the institutions solely through donation collections. From 1897 to 1942, thus long after his death, both of the still operating homes were located in a building at Schönhauser Allee 162, diagonally across from the cemetery. The last children and their teachers were deported to the death camps.

Located at the corner of field A is the double grave of two politicians and close friends, **Eduard Lasker** (1829–1884) and **Ludwig Bamberger** (1823–1899). A stone was erected between two columns, the German inscription of which reads: "Here rest united in death they who were united in life by a shared striving for Germany's unity and freedom." Lasker was born in Posen and studied law in Breslau. Along with Bamberger, he was one of the founders of the National Liberal Party and elected its chairman. He was a member of the Prussian parliament and, like Bamberger, also of the German Reichstag. In their capacity as parliamentarians, both men took part in the formulation of a law from 1876 which enabled the withdrawal from the Jewish community without conversion. In protest against the National Liberal Party's yielding to the restrictive policy pursued by Bismarck, they left the party – once again together – in 1880.

Behind the intersection, the honor row continues with field B. Here lies the grave of the literary scholar **Ludwig Geiger** (1848–1920), son of the Liberal rabbi Abraham Geiger. Among many other works he wrote a history of Jews in Berlin, still worth reading today, and was editor of numerous journals, including the *Goethe Yearbooks*.

Following this path, we reach the grave of **Leopold Zunz** (1794–1886), the founder of the Science of Judaism. He was born as Jom Tow Lipmann in Detmold, Westphalia. From 1815 to 1819 he studied at the University of Berlin, before he founded with Eduard Gans the Society for the Culture and Science of Jews in 1819. In 1821 Zunz received his doctorate in philosophy at the University of Halle (Saale). Again in Berlin, he worked for a time as a journalist and was director of the Jewish community school, later the Jewish teachers' seminar as well. His petition to have a chair for the Science of Judaism established at a German university was rejected. From this time on he devoted himself to his studies, in particular the Hebrew liturgy and synagogal poetry. His wife Adelheid (1802–1874) was buried beside him; she hosted a literary salon for over fifty years.

The next grave is that of the rabbi **Abraham Geiger** (1810–1874). He was a staunch advocate of Reform Judaism and was appointed rabbi in Berlin first in 1870. He was involved in the founding of the College for the Science of Judaism and taught there during the final two years of his life.

At the end of the path, we continue on the right, following the cemetery wall. After about fifty meters, the Beer family grave lies on the left, a classical wall vault with a raised back wall and lower wings. The most famous scion of this family is undoubtedly the composer **Giacomo Meyerbeer** (1791–1864). His marble memorial slab is on a pedestal and leans against the right wing of the vault. The grave was restored on the anniversary of Meyerbeer's 200th birthday. Since then the replicas of antiquity amphorae stand once more on the walls. Giacomo Meyerbeer was born into a wealthy Jewish family of merchants as Jakob Liebmann Meyer Beer. The musical prodigy began studying composition with Carl Friedrich Zelter in 1805. After staying for almost ten years in Italy, as of 1825 Meyerbeer spent the larger part of each year in Paris where he enjoyed enormous success with his extravagantly staged operas. In 1842 he was appointed general music director of the Berlin Opera and lived in Pariser Platz 6a next to the Brandenburg Gate. Although he died in Paris, Meyerbeer was buried in Berlin.

Some forty meters further on, to the left, we find the grave of **David Friedländer** (1750–1834), the co-founder and director of the Jewish Free School and the first Jewish city councilor in Berlin. Born in Königsberg, he came to Berlin in 1770 where he further developed the ideas of Moses Mendelssohn, translating the traditional prayer book into German.

Turning right at the end of the path, after some twenty meters along the cemetery wall we come across the Hirschfeld family grave. The banker **Israel Hirschfeld** (1801–1866) commissioned Johann Heinrich Strack (1805–1880), a Schinkel pupil who also designed the Berlin Victory Column, with the building of a classical gravesite. The three-winged grave consists of plinth courses upon which Doric columns support an architrave decorated with laurel wreaths. An iron lattice once protected the gravestones on the path side. Today this is missing, as are the vases on the architrave.

Following the cemetery wall, we pass the closed second entrance to the cemetery, known as the gate to the "communication." Behind it is the so-called "walkway of the Jews", some 400 meters long and reconstructed in 2002. An information panel is fixed to the gate at Kollwitzplatz, which is adorned with a Star of David. At the gate to the "communication," we find the grave of **Joseph Mendelssohn** (1770–1848). Together with his brother Abraham, the eldest son of Moses Mendelssohn founded the banking house J. & A. Mendelssohn in 1804. In 1815 the seat of the bank was moved to Jägerstrasse 51 where today a memorial plaque recalls the history of the bank.

Continuing in the same direction, we find on the right of the next junction in field E the Liebermann family grave, where the painter **Max Liebermann** (1847–1935) is also buried. The L-shaped plot in the Neo-Renaissance style was designed by the architect Hans Grisebach. The inscription in German Gothic on Max Liebermann's grave slab is taken from the Biblical story of Jacob's struggle with the angel. Also buried here are his parents, his brother Georg and his wife Martha, who, faced with imminent deportation in 1943, chose to commit suicide. After studying art in Weimar, Max Liebermann was one of the founding members of the Berlin Secession. In 1920 he was elected president of the Prussian Arts Academy. The National Socialists ousted him from all his posts as early as May 2, 1933, and his work was removed from all German museums. The Liebermann home at Pariser Platz 7, next to the Brandenburg Gate where Liebermann lived until his death, was completely destroyed in the Second World War. It has since been "critically reconstructed" following plans drafted by Joseph Paul Kleihues. Liebermann's summer house at the Grosser Wannsee, on Colomierstrasse 3, built in 1909 by Paul Baumgarten, is once more open to visitors. In its garden designed by Alfred Lichtwark, Liebermann painted and drew countless impressions of the splendid waterfront property. After his death the house was confiscated and used first by the German Reich Post and later as a hospital. Most recently it served as a clubhouse for scuba divers, who could only be persuaded to a property exchange after long negotiations. After years of effort, the Liebermann Society was finally able to take responsibility for the house in September 2002. By the end of 2004, around 30,000 visitors had admired the partially restored garden and the villa on weekends. Reconstruction work will be complete by mid-2005.

A detour into field E leads us to the grave of **Leopold Ullstein** (1826–1899). For Ullstein and his two wives buried next to him, very plain, reddish granite gravestones were erected with brief gilded inscriptions. Born in Fürth, Leopold Ullstein founded a publishing house in Berlin in 1877, which brought out the *Berliner Zeitung*. The *Berliner Morgenpost*, in publication since 1898 and initially published by his five sons, was for a time the German daily with the highest circulation.

Back to the path leading along the cemetery wall, at the next junction we reach the corner plot of field G. Here we find one of the most conspicuous graves, that of **Sophie Loewe** (1847–1876). A pyramid was erected in her honor, which upon closer inspection turns out to be a low relief. A medallion with her portrait in three-quarter profile, bordered by a wreath, is mounted on the pyramid above a suggested gate. The portrait is the earliest example in Berlin of the rare violation of the prohibition placed on graven images in Jewish cemeteries. The inscribed grave slab is set in the suggested gate. Also unusual is that the German inscription includes the date of marriage. With this gesture, her husband **Ludwig Loewe** (1837–1886), who is buried opposite, wanted to express the pain he felt at losing his young wife after only nine years of marriage. Loewe was not only a successful industrialist, but also Ferdinand Lassalle's private secretary for a time.

The last grave (on the left) on the cemetery wall is that of the couple **Bertha** (1837–1918) and **Moritz Manheimer** (1826–1916), who donated the financing for the former Jewish old age home, located directly behind the cemetery wall. The stone grave is decorated with an elaborately designed middle-section, in which a niche with a vase is mounted, and columns joined together by round arches.

The cemetery entrance is on the right.

CEMETERY AT HERBERT-BAUM-STRASSE 45 (WEISSENSEE)

Open: Sunday–Thursday 7 am–5 pm, in winter until 4 pm,
Friday 7 am–3 pm

As the Berlin Jewish community's numbers rose to 65,000 by 1875, it was clear that the cemetery on Schönhauser Allee would soon reach the limits of its capacity. The community therefore purchased a sufficiently large new property, covering a total of forty-three hectares. In 1878 the community exclusively invited members of the Berlin Architects' Association to take part in a competition for designing the cemetery. **Hugo Licht**, later city planning councilor and professor for architecture in Leipzig, was entrusted with the task.

The Jewish cemetery in Weissensee was officially opened on September 22, 1880. The cemetery grounds are divided exactly into geometrical fields, which are clearly marked with letters and numbers. For the entrance area Licht designed a mourning hall, a clinker-brick building in neo-Renaissance style. The actual mourning hall, located at the back of the building, is erected on a square ground plan as a

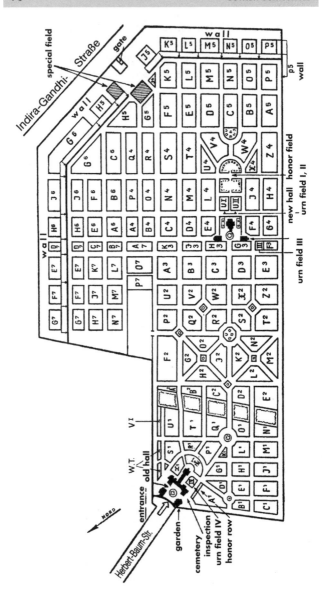

central building with an octagonal tambour. The cemetery grounds represent a veritable necropolis: a city of the dead with splendid avenues, byroads, lanes, squares, circular flowerbeds and intersecting paths.

A nursery with greenhouses was laid to offer visitors wreaths and flowers, although this is not really a part of the Jewish cemetery tradition. After the National Socialist seizure of power, numerous Jews were retrained here as gardeners and farmers before immigrating, so as to ensure for themselves work in the countries of exile, above all in Palestine.

In 1910 the building of a second mourning hall was necessary, for at this point in time an average of five to six funerals per day were being held at this cemetery alone. Beginning in 1914 an honor grove was planted for the Jewish soldiers who had fallen in the First World War, which was then given a more formal design by the community's master builder Alexander Beer in 1927. The whole area is set off from the rest of the cemetery by a two-meter high wall. The three-meter high central monument made of seashell limestone represents an altar. The paved square around the memorial is surrounded by uniform, low gravestones, which are inscribed only with the names and dates of the fallen.

After fierce debate and a community resolution, cremations were finally permitted, previously uncustomary in Judaism. As of 1926, the ashes of the dead were installed on specially laid out urn fields.

The Jewish cemetery in Weissensee was – besides the Jewish hospital on Exerzierstrasse in Wedding – the last Jewish institution that remained under Jewish administration until the end of the National Socialist dictatorship and persecution. Of all places, Jewish life continued on a cemetery. Not only were the deceased buried here according to Jewish rites, but Martin Riesenburger held secret religious services on Jewish holidays. Arthur Brass, at the time head of the cemetery administration, recalls that between "1938 and 1945 the Gestapo did not carry out any controls of the cemetery grounds and the buildings on the cemetery." Jews who had lived illegally in the city were thus sometimes able to hide on the cemetery grounds.

During the deportations the number of suicides rose dramatically. In 1942 alone, 811 people who committed suicide were buried here.

The grave fields in section 7 were laid out for the urns which were sent back from the concentration camps. Some 4,000 graves, the second mourning hall and the greenhouses were destroyed in air raids during the Second World War.

Immediately after the end of the war, Riesenburger held the first legal Jewish religious service in Berlin at this cemetery. Members of the West Berlin Jewish community were also buried here until the Jewish cemetery on Heerstrasse was opened. The severely decimated community saw itself unable to prevent the cemetery from falling into neglect. In the GDR, where officially antisemitism was non-existent, graves were desecrated as early as the late 1950s and again in the 1980s.

The cemetery inspector keeps a funeral and grave plot register, in which up to the present day over 115,000 graves are listed. The Weissensee cemetery is thus one of the largest Jewish cemeteries in Europe. Since only around 1,500 gravesites are cared for by the few relatives and survivors of the Shoah who still reside in Berlin, the limited number of cemetery employees are completely overburdened. Especially in the areas farthest away from the large avenues, vast sections of the cemetery are overgrown. The community invests 800,000 Euros annually for the upkeep of the enormous area. Because the cemetery is classified as a historical monument, the Berlin Senate provides some financial subsidies. The Federal Government and the Federal Armed Forces also contribute financially to the restoration of graves.

The most recent example of the numerous attacks by rightwing extremists on this cemetery took place at the beginning of October 1999, when unknown culprits overturned 103 gravestones, many of which were irreparably destroyed. A new security concept for the cemetery was discussed in talks held between the community, the state security authorities, the police and the Berlin Senate.

Using the ground plan (page 70), it is not difficult to find one's way through the large cemetery. Beginning at the honor row that extends from field A1 to field G1, the description of the graves' arrangement leads us from the entrance area deep into the cemetery grounds. Only a few of the well-known Jewish personalities buried here are singled out.

In the middle of the circular flowerbed at the entrance area stands a memorial stone for the Jews murdered between 1933 and 1945. On a circular strip of lawn surrounding the stone are smaller memorial stones inscribed with the names of the largest concentration camps.

A path on our right leads to the honor row, which was laid out in the first row of the fields A1 and G1.

The very plain grave of the scholar **David Cassel** (1818–1893) is the first we encounter here. A lecturer at the College for the Science of Judaism, Cassel was also a co-founder of the Jewish Students Aid Association and was director of the "Dina Nauen School for Orphans" in Berlin for over thirty years.

The pale gravestone erected for **Louis Lewandowski** (1821–1894) and his wife is made up of a terraced plinth, base and triangular pediment. A black inscription tablet ends with the motto: "Love makes the hymn immortal." Louis Lewandowski is regarded as one of the founders of modern synagogue music. Born in Wreschen (Posen) in 1821, at the age of twelve he arrived in Berlin penniless. Besides organ and choral music, he composed the liturgy of the Liberal rite, thus contributing decisively to the development and establishment of Reform Judaism. He was the first cantor of the New Synagogue on the Oranienburger Strasse.

The scholar and important representative of the Science of Judaism, **Moritz Steinschneider** (1816–1907) worked mainly in the area of bibliography, focusing on Hebrew manuscripts and printed works. He saw himself as a kind of gravedigger, preparing an "honorable burial" for the history of Hebrew literature, which he considered to have reached its conclusion. He died without having to endure the catastrophic end of the deceptive German-Jewish symbiosis and without being able to marvel at the remarkable revival of Hebrew literature. The granite stone decorated with a Star of David and two palm leaves is dedicated to him and his wife.

The rabbi **Martin Riesenburger** (1896–1965) worked in the Jewish home for the elderly on Grosse Hamburger Strasse from 1933 until the Gestapo converted it into a collection camp. He then continued his spiritual welfare work at the Weissensee cemetery, conducting funerals and, from time to time, even holding secret religious services. He also courageously helped to hide both Jews who had gone underground and Torah scrolls that had been rescued. On May 11, 1945, he held the first religious services after the war here at this cemetery. In the GDR he was the head rabbi to the Jewish communities in East Germany.

We have now reached the honor row on field G1. A sarcophagus, rare in Weissensee, decorates the grave of the philosopher **Hermann Cohen** (1842–1918), a key figure of the neo-Kantian Marburg School. The priest's hands raised in blessing in the gable wall refer to the name Cohen, which means priest. After attaining emeritus status, towards the end of his life Cohen moved to Berlin to intensify his studies and his analysis of the Jewish religion. He taught at the College for the Science of Judaism and worked on his late principal work *The Religion of Reason. Out of the Sources of Judaism*, which was first published posthumously.

The grave of **Micha Josef Bin-Gorion** (1865–1921) comprises of a gable-peaked stele made of seashell limestone. It displays an exceptionally successful typography of Hebrew letters. A lion poised to leap refers to the somewhat unusual vocalized Hebrew surname. Born Berdyczewski, he first adopted this name when he began his efforts to revive Hebrew as a literary language. Bin-Gorion became popular through his collections of Jewish legends and stories, which he published under the titles *The Fount Judas* and *The Legends of the Jews*.

Located on the opposite side on the path is a gravestone that stands alone, erected in honor of the communist resistance activist **Herbert Baum** (1912–1942). Having joined the German Communist Youth League in 1932, together with his wife **Marianne Baum** (1912–1942) he led a communist resistance group that as of 1936 was made up almost entirely of young Jews. Besides spreading fliers, they also established contact to French and Belgian forced laborers. On May 18, 1942, the group laid an incendiary device in the propaganda exhibition "The Soviet Paradise," which was being held in a building specially erected for the exhibition on the Lustgarten in front of the Old Museum (in Mitte). The National Socialists brutally avenged this largely ineffective operation. They arrested 154 uninvolved Jews, who were then executed at the Sachsenhausen concentration camp along with a further ninety-six camp prisoners. The families of these 250 executed Jews were taken to the Theresienstadt concentration camp, from where most of them were then deported to the mass death camps. In the same year, twenty-eight members of the resistance group, with an average age of 22, were arrested, sentenced to death and executed at Plötzensee. The rear of the black granite stone lists the names and young ages of the executed members of the Herbert Baum group. Not far away, on field Z1, are the graves of **Richard** (1911–1975) and **Charlotte Holzer** (1909–1980), who were the only members of the resistance group not to be murdered. In 1981, on May 8, the official day in the GDR for remembering the liberation from fascism, a cube-shaped memorial stone was erected at the edge of the Lustgarten. The street leading to the cemetery, Lothringenstrasse, was renamed Herbert-Baum-Strasse.

Returning to the honor row, we find the grave of the Impressionist painter and graphic artist **Lesser Ury** (1861–1931), whose gravestone captivates through its unadorned, modern design. Except for the Hebrew concluding phrase, which here is unusually set at the beginning, the inscription is in German. Ury was denied all of his life the critical and public acclaim he deserved, partially due to his earlier disputes with the more influential Max Liebermann.

No longer buried in the honor row but off the path at the tenth row in field A1 is the journalist and man of letters **Theodor Wolff** (1868–1943). In 1894 he became Paris correspondent for the *Berliner Tageblatt* and together with Emile Zola and Anatole France supported the rehabilitation of Captain Dreyfus, a Jew who had been falsely accused of treason. By 1906 editor-in-chief of the *Tageblatt*, Wolff was one of the most important journalists in the Weimar Republic. Immediately after Hitler seized power, he wrote an editorial calling for resistance against the National Socialists. He fled Germany on the night of the Reichstag fire, but was arrested ten years later by the Gestapo in Nice. Aged 75, he had to endure stays in several prisons and the Sachsenhausen concentration camp before he died, completely enfeebled, in the Jewish hospital in Wedding.

Opposite field M1 at the cemetery wall we find the family mausoleum of the publisher **Rudolf Mosse** (1843–1920). The classicist vault of red granite is a typical example of the adoption of Antique forms while simultaneously abstaining from the use of Jewish symbolism and epigraphy. In 1872 Mosse founded a newspaper publisher that brought out the *Berliner Tageblatt*, the *Berliner Morgenpost*, the *Berliner Volkszeitung*, the *8-Uhr-Abendblatt* and a few magazines. After his death the company's headquarters, the Mosse House at Schützenstrasse 15–18 (Mitte), was rebuilt and extended by Erich Mendelsohn and Richard Neutra. The impressive architectural monument can still be admired today. The National Socialists expropriated the company in 1933.

Buried on field U1 in row 11 is **Lina Morgenstern** (1830–1909). She was popularly known as "soup Lina," an appropriate and endearing name, for she had set up a series of soup kitchens. The extremely committed social worker founded various charitable associations. The brief inscription on the gravestone, which she shares with her husband, extols her as a "great philanthropist." An honor wreath decorates the rounded gable of the granite stone.

On field C2, at the circular flowerbed, we find the family grave of the banker **Sigmund Aschrott** (1826–1915). The Royal Prussian Councilor of Commerce originally had the mausoleum, once of reddish granite but now strongly darkened, erected for his wife Anna. The plans were drawn up by Bruno Schmitz, the architect of the Battle of the Nations monument in Leipzig. A Star of David, serving as a source of light from above, adorns the pyramid-shaped roof. The colossal vault gives the impression nevertheless of an expensive but at the same time tasteless turn away from Jewish grave art.

The plain family graves of the entrepreneurs **Hermann Tietz** (1837–1907) and **Oskar Tietz** (1858–1923) are located on field 02, opposite field G2. In 1882 they opened a small linen business in Gera. They achieved their commercial breakthrough with low and fixed prices, by offering a wide array of goods, clever advertising and by gradually founding a chain of department stores that became increasingly representative. By 1900 the first Tietz emporium was opened in Berlin on Leipziger Strasse, which was soon followed by two more. After the death of his uncle, Oskar Tietz ran the business. After acquiring the "Kaufhaus des Westens" (KaDeWe) in 1926, the firm "Hermann Tietz" became the largest department store group in Europe. In 1934 the company was forcibly "Aryanized." Since then the department stores carry the name "Hertie", formed from the first letters of the founders' first and surnames.

On field T2, at the flowerbed, we see the family grave of the gastronome **Berthold Kempinski** (1845–1910). It is made up of a row of columns which is enclosed with grave slabs and, arch-shaped, forms the rear of the cemetery property. A medallion with a portrait of Kempinski is seen on the large decorated urn, which is positioned on a freestanding column ruin. In 1873, a year after his arrival in Berlin, Kempinski opened his first wine store at Friedrichstrasse 178. There then followed a variety of other business ventures, such as a mail-order service for wine, a delicatessen, a wine warehouse and wine restaurant at Kurfürstendamm 27, on the corner of Fasanenstrasse. The Hotel Kempinski, which although it bears the old name was "Aryanized" by the National Socialists, is located here today. The members of the Kempinski family either fled Germany or were murdered.

Opposite field T2, at the enclosing wall, is the family grave of the entrepreneur **Adolf Jandorf** (1870–1932). After becoming familiar with the sales techniques used in the U. S. A. during a trip there, in 1892 Jandorf opened his first department store based on the American model in Berlin on the Spittelmarkt (Mitte). Five others were to follow, including the "Kaufhaus des Westens" (KaDeWe) in 1907.

On the corner plot of field D4, in the direction of C4 and M4, we find the family grave of the cigarette manufacturer **Josef Garbáty-Rosenthal** (1851–1939). The almost enclosed, classical gravesite is made up of a slightly curving row of columns which run out and forward into lower side walls. The rear wall is dominated by two pairs of Doric columns bearing a terraced gable inscribed with the family names. The successful manufacturer was a generous donator, helping to establish for example the synagogue in the Jewish orphanage in Pankow, a chair at the College for the Science of Judaism and various social and leisure-time organizations for his employees. The family's possessions were expropriated in 1938 and the firm "Aryanized." The sons were able to immigrate with their families to the United States. The 88-year-old head of the family remained in Germany and died a year later.

On field J4, opposite the urn graves on the honor field, are the graves of the publisher **Samuel Fischer** (1859–1934) and his family. The plain gravestone is decorated with the well-known firm logo. After completing training as a book seller in Vienna, Fischer moved to

Berlin in 1881. He founded the S. Fischer publishing house in 1886, publishing and promoting mainly authors who were part of the Naturalism movement and socially critical, like Henrik Ibsen, Emile Zola and Gerhart Hauptmann. He also acquired writers who were less well-known at the time, such as Thomas Mann, Jakob Wassermann, Franz Kafka, Stefan Zweig and Hermann Hesse. As of 1905 Samuel Fischer lived at Erdener Strasse 8 in an art nouveau villa where today a memorial plaque with a silhouette commemorates the former resident. Samuel Fischer's son-in-law, Gottfried Bermann-Fischer (1897–1995), took over the directorship of the publishing house in 1932. In 1936 the firm was forced to move, first to Vienna, two years later to Stockholm and finally to New York in 1940. Since 1950 the firm's headquarters have been located in Frankfurt am Main; in the 1990s an office was once again opened in Berlin that organizes readings and lectures.

In field P4 stands a slim and very plain gravestone, rounded at the top, which was erected for **Moritz Heimann** (1868–1925), the chief editor who rendered outstanding service to the S. Fischer Verlag.

Also on field P4, opposite field O4, we find the grave of the businessman **Albert Mendel** (1866–1922). The plan for the grave, still remarkably modern in its appearance today, was drawn up by the path-breaking Bauhaus architect Walter Gropius (1883–1969), who had also previously designed the interior of Mendel's home at Lützowplatz. Erected in 1924, the asymmetrical grave is made up of a back, framed along the top and down the right side, and a stylized, completely undecorated and austere sarcophagus that stands diagonally in front of it.

Also worth looking for is the gravestone of the government architect **Louis Fränkel** (1863–1922) on field F5 in row 19. The expressive grave is made up of seven slabs, tapering off at the top, which, standing behind one another, increase in size and vaguely recall the covenant tablets. The front and smallest slab bears the names of Louis Fränkel and his wife and their dates of birth and death. The second, much larger slab is decorated with a Star of David. The whole grave stands on a five-stepped pedestal. It represents an extremely successful example of the attempt to employ a modern language of form while referring at the same time to Jewish tradition. The latter aspect is ensured through the number and shape of the individual elements, the flow of the visual line pointing upwards and the Star of David.

On field G5 we find the grave of the Scholem family. Only the head of the family, Arthur Scholem (1863–1925), owner of a printing business, actually found his lasting resting place here. The most famous son of this fully assimilated Berlin family is the scholar **Gerhard Gershom Scholem** (1897–1982). The ardent Zionist migrated to Palestine immediately after completing his doctorate in Munich in 1923, taking up a post as professor at the newly founded Hebrew University in Jerusalem. Scholem was the first to undertake scholarly research into the Kabbalah, the mystic-theosophical Jewish occult doctrine. Over eighty years old, he took up an invitation to be the first fellow of the newly established Institute for Advanced Studies in Berlin, only to become ill during the unaccustomed winter. He died shortly after returning to Jerusalem, where he was buried. Despite her advanced years, his mother Betty Scholem (1866–1946) followed her son Erich Scholem (1893–1965) into exile in Australia in 1939, where she died and was buried. A further son, the communist and Reichstag deputy Werner Scholem (1895–1942), was murdered in the Buchenwald concentration camp.

The mausoleum of the renowned singer **Joseph Schwarz** (1881–1926) on field A6, opposite field E6, has the form of a Greek temple. Doric columns carry a decorated architrave upon which a saddleback roof, completed by a triangular gable, rests. The open gravesite is closed solely by the rear wall that is broken by openings for light and on whose inner side stands the deceased's name. Located in the interior is a classically shaped block of stone that is inscribed on its front with the Psalm verse, "Lord, thou are my refuge for ever and ever." During the Second World War the grave itself served as a refuge for Jews who had gone underground; the roof construction provided them with a hideout at night.

ADASS YISROEL CEMETERY

Wittlicher Strasse 2 (previously Falkenberger Chaussee; Weissensee),
Tel. 925 17 24
Open: Visits must be scheduled in advance by telephone,
Tel. 281 31 35

One of the first concerns of the newly founded independent Adass
Yisroel community was to establish its own cemetery since the many
changes adopted by Reform Judaism that were not accepted by the
Orthodox Jews also affected the cemetery. To counter this development, the separate congregation created its own "Cemetery and Burial Rules", which specified the exact observance of the religious laws:
no grave decorations, no flowers or wreathes, a white burial shroud
and no prestigious family graves. Non-Hebrew inscriptions are only
permitted on the backside of the gravestone, which are to be placed in
front of the wooden coffin.

The community purchased this property of about two hectares on
December 22, 1873. The first congregation member, Abraham Michel-
son, was not buried at the new cemetery until 1880 (field A, row 1).
An independent burial fraternity, a *Hevrah Kaddisha,* was founded in
1890. The cemetery contains about 3,000 burial plots.

The cemetery was hardly damaged during the years of National
Socialism. Only the ceremony hall to the left of the entrance was
hit by bombs and had to be torn down after the war. After 1974
the cemetery was cared for by the cemetery attendant Arthur Sterr.
After he retired, the cemetery on Herbert-Baum-Strasse took over
its administration. About a third of the grounds that had not been
parceled out was sold. The cemetery, left to its own fate, fell into neglect and was overgrown. For a while a hole in the damaged wall
around the grounds made it possible for people from the neighboring area to enter the cemetery and destroy over 2,000 gravestones.
Hundreds of headstones disappeared. The cemetery wall was later
repaired and a new attendant's house was erected to the right of the
entrance. The cemetery was rededicated on June 26, 1986 with a
ceremony attended by former community members from all over the
world.

Two memorial stones have been placed just behind the entrance. The right stone is a monument to the approximately ninety desecrated Torah scrolls. They were part of a convolute of what had once been 583 Torah scrolls from the dissolved Jewish communities of Prussia that the National Socialists stole for an anti-Jewish incitement exhibition they were planning to present in the synagogue at Münchener Strasse 37. They had been stored temporarily in the Israelite Hospital. Arthur Brass, the head of the cemetery administration at the time, and a few helpers secretly moved them from there to the cemetery of the main community in Weissensee and hid them in the New Hall and in a neighboring building. Unfortunately, the New Hall was hit by bombs in the summer of 1943. The ninety or so destroyed scrolls were buried in the Adass Yisroel cemetery. After the war, the 500 Torah scrolls that were rescued were distributed to newly founded synagogues in Germany and other European countries.

The stone on the left was set up in honor of the re-dedication in 1986 and on its front side, in Hebrew and in German, the members of the congregation who were murdered by the National Socialists are commemorated. A few names are listed on the back to symbolically represent all the victims.

The cemetery is divided into lettered sections (A-G) that are designated by signs. Because all the gravestones, with few exceptions, were kept at equal height, the cemetery is less interesting to people fascinated by sepulchers. But unlike the external grave designs, the Hebrew inscriptions are very diverse and characteristic. Depending on the degree of interest, it is worthwhile getting a general overview of the grounds by staying on the main paths or to walk along the narrow numbered rows and explore the various gravestones.

The left corner of the cemetery grounds on Wittlicher Strasse contains about 200 graves from the second Spandau cemetery that was established in 1859. In the spring of 1940 its property had to be sold to the Wehrmacht and the deceased were reburied at the Adass Yisroel cemetery. Even the gravestones were moved to the new location – no doubt the only time that ever occurred during the Nazi era.

A number of well-known people were buried at the Adass Yisroel cemetery. In the first row of each respective field and hence easy to locate are the graves of Esriel Hildesheimer, David Hoffmann, Hirsch Hildesheimer, Meir Hildesheimer, Salomon Winter and the Schocken family.

Born into a family of scholars, the later rabbi **Esriel Hildesheimer** (1820–1899) attended the Jewish school in his hometown of Halberstadt. He studied Semitic languages, philosophy, history and natural sciences at the university in Berlin. After completing his rabbinical training, he served as a rabbi in Eisenstadt in Austria. The curriculum of the *Yeshivah* (in English: "Talmud school") founded by Hildesheimer also included secular fields. Hildesheimer was the first rabbi of the newly founded Adass Yisroel congregation. One of his first acts was to found the Orthodox Rabbinical Seminary. The students, who were simultaneously enrolled at the university, also focused on modern scholarly disciplines.

After the death of Esriel Hildesheimer, Prof. Dr. **David Hoffmann** (1843–1921) became the rector of the rabbinical seminary, primarily teaching the Torah and Talmud. Born in Slovakia, Hoffmann had been a pupil of Hildesheimer back in Eisenstadt and was considered to be equally broadly educated. Towards the end of his life he was recognized by the Orthodox Jews in Germany as the leading authority on religious law. He was granted the honorary title of professor by the German government on his 75th birthday.

Hirsch Hildesheimer (1855–1910), the son of Esriel Hildesheimer, was instructor for Jewish history and Palestine geography at the rabbinical seminary. He studied history, philosophy and geography in Berlin and Leipzig and wrote his dissertation under the guidance of Theodor Mommsen, the author of *The History of the Romans*. In addition to teaching, he published a number of geographic and religious texts. He vehemently pushed for the recognition of ritual slaughter of animals as the best method.

The expressionist architect Erich Mendelsohn designed the gravestone of the **Schocken** family (field F, row 1), made of three pillars of white seashell limestone. In 1901 Simon Schocken, who died in 1929, and his brother Salman (1877–1959), who later became known as a bibliophile and publisher, founded a department store in Zwickau that expanded into one of the most successful department store chains in the Weimar Republic.

The sculptor **Jakob Plessner** (1871–1936) was buried in field D, row 1. He created numerous portrait busts, including one of Moses Mendelssohn, Oskar Tietz and the Great Elector.

The extremely popular acrobat and circus artist **Siegmund Breitbart** (1893–1925) was buried amidst tremendous public attention (field G, row 16). The Circus Busch proclaimed him to be the strongest man in the world. He bent iron rods and horseshoes, busted apart chains with his bare hands. Celebrated as the "Iron King," he made a career for himself in American shows. A scratch from a small, rusty nail proved the giant's undoing; he died of blood poisoning.

CEMETERY AT HEERSTRASSE/SCHOLZPLATZ

Heerstrasse 141 (Charlottenburg), Tel. 304 32 34
Open: Sunday–Thursday 7 am–5 pm, in winter until 4 pm,
Friday until 3 pm

In November 1955 a new cemetery was dedicated on the edge of Grunewald for the Jewish community in the west part of Berlin. The architect Kurt Lechnitzer and the landscape architect Bernhard Kynast designed the burial grounds. The entrance leads through an iron gate into a courtyard with the mortuary on the left and the administration building adjacent. A second gateway leads to the actual cemetery. The cemetery contains about 5,000 gravesites by now.

Four gravestones from Juden-Kiewer from Spandau stand on both sides of the middle path. They were discovered during restoration work in the Spandau Citadel. The middle path leads directly to the central memorial stone that was erected in 1960 to remember the Jews who were murdered in the Shoah. Ashes from the Auschwitz concentration camp were buried in front of the monument designed by Josef M. Lellek and made of stones from the destroyed synagogue on Fasanenstrasse. This is also where the cross axis intersects with the honorary row, and where Heinz Galinski – right at the entrance – and behind him, Jeanette Wolff and Estrongo Nachama are buried along side others.

Heinz Galinski (1912–1992) was born in Marienburg. In 1938 he was forced to do slave labor in Berlin and in early February 1943 was deported from the Grunewald depot station to Auschwitz. He lost his entire family in the Shoah. He was liberated from the Bergen-Belsen concentration camp in April 1945. From 1949 until his death he served as chairman of the Jewish Community of Berlin or rather, of West Berlin, and was at the same time chairman of the Central Council of Jews in Germany. Galinski worked vehemently his entire life for the re-establishment of the Jewish community in Germany and sharply criticized antisemitic incidents. He rendered outstanding work in the negotiations for the immigration of Jews from the former Soviet Union to Germany. His grave was vandalized by rightwing extremists and the grave plate blown up on December 19, 1998. The ruins, placed next to the new grave plate that was later erected, were preserved to serve as an admonishment.

The representative of the Social Democratic Party **Jeanette Wolff** (1888–1976) spent the entire Nazi era in prisons and concentration camps. Her entire family was murdered. Nevertheless she worked tirelessly after the war for the development of democracy in West Germany, ultimately as a deputy in the federal parliament. She served in Berlin on the city council and was elected to the Berlin House of Representatives. She became chairman of the (West) Berlin Jewish Community Board and Central Welfare Office.

Estrongo Nachama (1918–2000) was born in Saloniki, Greece. He survived a number of concentration camps and death marches. Although his entire family was murdered in Auschwitz, he chose to stay in Germany after he was liberated near Berlin in 1945. With his wonderful voice Nachama became head cantor in the Pestalozzistrasse synagogue and contributed largely to arranging its liturgy. His music became famous and he was invited to perform concerts throughout the world. He worked hard for the dialogue between Jews and Christians and performed in Christian churches. He also made a name for himself when the Berlin Wall still stood by crossing the border to visit the East Berlin Jewish community on holidays and on other special occasions such as weddings and funerals. His son Andreas Nachama was chairman of the Jewish Community of Berlin from 1997 to 2001.

The actor **Ernst Deutsch** (1890–1969), who was born in Prague and became one of the most well-known theater actors of his time in Germany, is buried in field WI. His grave is surrounded by a tall hedge. Max Reinhardt employed Deutsch from 1917 to 1921 at the Deutsches Theater in Berlin. In the early 1930s he performed at the Viennese Burgtheater. During the period of National Socialism Deutsch emigrated via England to the United States and Argentina. In 1947 he returned to (West) Berlin and gave very impressive renditions both of Nathan in *Nathan the Wise* and of Shylock in *The Merchant of Venice*.

The grave of **Julius Klausner** (1874–1950), entwined in ivy, lies in field BII, row 1. His shoe store chain is still well-known in Berlin under the name Leiser, which was the maiden name of his wife Dora (1882–1959). Before 1933 the company had thirty-three branches in Berlin alone. After Julius Klausner was arrested for a short time in 1935, he was forced to sell a quarter of his business. Further forced sales followed in 1937. The couple immigrated via the Netherlands to Argentina. The business was returned to Klausner after the war, after which he re-sold it. Julius Klausner died in 1950 in Buenos Aires. His wife returned to Berlin and had the remains of her deceased husband transferred to Berlin and reburied in the newly opened Heerstrasse cemetery.

The Shoah –
Memorials and Monuments

THE ANNIHILATION OF JEWISH LIFE IN BERLIN BY THE NATIONAL SOCIALISTS

The Hebrew term *Shoah*, which translated means "catastrophe" or "destruction" in English, stands for what was done to the Jews between 1933 and 1945. The systematically organized and technological mass murder of millions of Jews from all over Europe is better conveyed by this term, which Jews also use, than the oft used word "Holocaust." The Greek word became known through the American television series of the same name and originally signified a sacrificial burnt offering.

Berlin, the capital of the Reich, was the seat of the government and also home to ministries, organizations, institutions and official agencies that were involved in the disenfranchisement, expulsion and annihilation of European Jewry. Unscrupulous administrative killers such as Hitler, Himmler, Heydrich, Kaltenbrunner and Eichmann ordered and organized the genocide of millions of people. The gradual exclusion of Jews from German society under the premise of a legal state is illustrated, for example, by the signs citing anti-Jewish legislation that hang on street masts throughout the Bayerisches Viertel in Berlin. Numerous forced labor camps, concentration camp subcamps, collection sites for Jews awaiting their deportation or for their possessions were also set up at many locations throughout the city. In many cases Jewish community institutions were misused for this purpose. The Sachsenhausen and Ravensbrück concentration camps are located not far from Berlin.

The infamous Nuremberg Race Laws were passed in 1935. Afterwards the Berlin Building Association evicted their Jewish tenants; park benches bore the inscription: "For Jews Only" and large numbers of shops, restaurants and even towns hung signs announcing that

Jews were "unwanted." This clearly visible public expression of racism was discontinued for a short time during the 1936 Olympic Games in Berlin.

On March 28, 1938 the Jewish community lost its status as a recognized public body and was reduced to a private institution. The pogrom that took place during the night of November 9, 1938 signified a dramatic turning point in the history of National Socialist policies of persecution. Many synagogues and private places of worship were set on fire or demolished. Approximately 10,000 Jews from Berlin and elsewhere were incarcerated in the Sachsenshausen concentration camp. After most rabbis had immigrated, only Leo Baeck (who survived in Theresienstadt), Felix Singerman (who was murdered in Riga in 1942) and Martin Salomonski (who was murdered in 1944 in Auschwitz) continued to serve as spiritual leaders for the remaining third of the Berlin Jewish community.

On January 24, 1939 the Gestapo set up the "Central Office for Jewish Emigration" in Berlin to assist in the legal emigration of Jews from Germany. Emigration was banned on October 23, 1941.

With the start of World War II, Jews were forced to do slave labor. To this end an "Employment Office for Jewish Workers" was established on January 31, 1940. The first collection camp for 1,000 people was set up in the synagogue on Levetzowstrasse; others were established later in various institutions of the Jewish community. Deportation trains from Berlin went first to Riga, Minsk, Kovno, Lodz, Lublin, Theresienstadt, Auschwitz and Tallinn. Later they departed for Bergen-Belsen, Ravensbrück and Sachsenshausen. On a total of sixty-three "East Transports," 35,000 Jews were deported to extermination camps in the east. Ninety-five percent of them were murdered. On 117 so-called "Elderly Transports" approximately 15,000 for the most part elderly Jews were deported to Theresienstadt; ninety percent of them did not survive. By the spring of 1942, only forced laborers who were working in armaments production and indispensable employees of the community were spared deportation. On June 10, 1943 the Gestapo closed down all the Jewish community institutions. Jewish protest or resistance against the National Socialist regime was hardly possible given the rigorously organized anti-Jewish policies. The few examples of resistance include the Herbert Baum communist resistance group's arson attack on the propaganda exhibition in the Berlin Lustgarten and the women's protest on Rosenstrasse against what is known as the "Factory Action." Far too few non-Jewish citizens helped Jews escape deportation. One exception is the Berliner Otto Weidt.

The National Socialists declared Berlin to be officially "free of Jews" on June 16, 1943. In truth, a few thousand Jews still lived in the city. They were either interned in the Jewish Hospital in Wedding or worked at the Jewish Cemetery in Weissensee. Many thousands of Jews lived illegally in hiding or with false papers in Berlin.

A number of commemorative sites in Berlin recall the terrible events of this period.

Since 1996, every year on April 9 – the day the Shoah is commemorated in Israel – at different sites in Berlin such as the memorial stone at Grosse Hamburger Strasse, the Fasanenstrasse community center, and Wittenbergplatz, young schoolchildren read out the names of the 55,696 Berlin Jews who were murdered by the National Socialists.

"THE ABANDONED ROOM" MONUMENT FOR BERLIN JEWS WHO DIED IN THE SHOAH

Koppenplatz (Mitte)

A few park benches are set around the square next to a playground. At the center stands a parquet floor with a life-size table and two chairs cast in bronze. One of the chairs lies knocked over on the floor as if someone had jumped up in fear. There are no people or any other objects in sight. This very impressive monument is called "The Abandoned Room" and commemorates the Berlin Jews who were murdered by the National Socialists. In 1988, for the 50th anniversary of the November pogrom, a competition was conducted by the East Berlin magistrate for a site to commemorate the Berlin Jews. The winning design by **Carl Biedermann** and **Eva Butzmann** was not realized until 1996. The inscription that runs along the floor plate of the monument comes from a poem by Nelly Sachs, winner of the Nobel Prize for Literature.

"The Abandoned Room" Monument

"Women's Block" Monument

DEPORTATION MONUMENT ON THE PUTLITZ BRIDGE (TIERGARTEN)

The Putlitz Bridge runs across the railroad tracks of the Moabit freight depot. Between 1941 and 1944 many Berlin Jews were deported from this station in cattle cars and brought to extermination camps in the East. In 1987 a sculpture by the sculptor **Volkmar Haase** was placed on the bridge as a memorial. An elongated broken plate protrudes out over the railing, symbolizing the path that victims took to the station on the way to their death. Symbolic broken steps are portrayed at the top of the sculpture. A second plate, half the size of the first and crowned by a Star of David, slants forward towards the viewer. An information panel placed under the star provides a short text on the history of this site.

The memorial has been repeatedly vandalized by rightwing extremists. Three times between 1989 and 1991 half of a pig's head was found here. On the night of April 20, 1992, Hitler's birthday, the monument was desecrated with the fecal matter of a man who was later apprehended. On August 29 of the same year a bomb went off badly damaging the memorial. It has meanwhile been repaired and a small panel was added which documents the last act of vandalism.

GRUNEWALD DEPORTATIONS MEMORIAL AND TRACK 17

At the Grunewald Station (Wilmersdorf)

Most of the Berlin Jews were deported from the Grunewald freight depot. The 35,000 people who were sent like cattle from here are commemorated by an eighteen meter long, three meter high concrete wall designed by the sculptor **Karol Bronitowski** in 1991. The wall is partly broken and its surface is full of cracks. Deep impressions of human silhouettes are set irregularly into it. An inscription on a column informs of the deportations.

Not far away, a second monument designed by **Nikolaus Hirsch**, **Wolfgang Lorch** and **Andrea Wandel**, titled "Track 17" was dedicated in 1998. Partly broken steel plates lie along both sides of a railroad track. A text provides information on the number of deported Jews, the date of each transport and its destination – the concentration camps and death camps.

JEWISH HOME FOR THE ELDERLY MEMORIAL STONE AND SCULPTURAL GROUP

Grosse Hamburger Strasse 26 (Mitte)

The simple, rectangular memorial stone on Hamburger Strasse commemorates the former Jewish Home for the Elderly that the Gestapo used in 1942 as a collection site for the Berlin Jews who were to be deported. Slightly hidden to the right of the stone stands the sculptural group originally designed by the sculptor **Will Lammert** (1892–1957) in 1957 for the Ravensbrück concentration camp for women. The women and girl figures are only a model of the work that was never realized. The East Germans who commissioned the piece carelessly dedicated the sculpture of female figures to all victims of fascism without making any reference to the home for the elderly and the Jews who were deported from here.

MEMORIAL FOR THE MURDERED JEWS OF EUROPE (HOLOCAUST MEMORIAL)

Ebertstrasse (Mitte)

The journalist Lea Rosh and the historian Eberhard Jäckel had the idea in 1988 to mobilize a citizen's initiative for a central monument dedicated to the Jews of Europe who were murdered by the National Socialists. A competition for the design was conducted in 1994–95 by the federal government, the state of Berlin and the sponsor association. Federal land was provided for the memorial right next to the Brandenburg Gate where the Berlin Wall used to stand. More than 500 architects and artists participated in the competition. The winning design, a slab as large as a soccer field with space for the names of six million Jewish victims was not realized because Helmut Kohl, federal chancellor at the time, exercised his veto.

A second competition held in October 1997 was won by a design created jointly by the New York architect **Peter Eisenman** and the American sculptor Richard Serra, which called for a field of 4,000 concrete steles. After the design was heavily criticized and declared a monstrosity, Serra – angered by the reaction – withdrew from the project. Eisenman later revised the design, reducing the number of steles to 2,711.

The Minister of Cultural Affairs at the time, Michael Naumann, suggested extending Eisenman's design to incorporate a "Site of Memory" that would include a documentation center, library and genocide research institute. This kind of documentation center already exists in Berlin, however, with the Topography of Terror, the Wannsee Conference House Memorial and the Center for Antisemitism Research at the Technische Universität.

The German Bundestag decided on June 25, 1999 with 314 "yes" votes to have the design from Eisenman built with the additional "Site of Information" made up of a number of rooms beneath the field of steles and covering an area of 800 square meters. In it the fate of fifteen representative families will be documented to represent the six million victims of the Shoah. It was also resolved that the monument should be dedicated solely to the European Jews and not generally to all victims of National Socialism.

Many people are reminded of a Jewish cemetery when they see the memorial design, but Eisenman compares it to a swaying cornfield. The rectangular steles stand up to four meters high and are placed a meter apart, distributed over an even grid. The grounds of the memorial slant down towards the center, lending the impression that visitors sink between the steles as they walk through the memorial. Its surface is sealed with a special material that allows for the anticipated right-wing graffiti to be easily removed.

The foundation stone was symbolically laid during a ceremony on January 27, 2000, the German memorial day for the victims of National Socialism. Dedicated on May 10, 2005, construction was supposed to have begun in autumn of 2002 and cost fifteen million

German Marks, but costs doubled partly due to the underground documentation center. The memorial is now said to have cost a total of 27.8 million Euros.

MIRROR WALL FOR THE JEWISH CITIZENS OF STEGLITZ

Hermann-Ehlers-Platz (Steglitz)

Hidden behind the bustle of a daily market and unnoticed by most of the passersby stands a mirror wall that commemorates the fate of the Jewish residents of the Steglitz district in Berlin. The memorial was based on a design by **Wolfgang Göschel**, **Joachim von Rosenberg** and **Hans-Norbert Burkert**. Eighteen mirrors of polished steel are engraved with the names and addresses of 1,723 deported Jews from Steglitz. The names of the deceased on the mirror fuse into the faces of people passing by and observers of the memorial. Detailed texts on the deportations and etched photographs of Berlin synagogues are integrated into the design.

Before the mirror wall was erected, there was a great deal of media attention paid to the protests of citizens groups and quarrels between district politicians. The mirror wall project was strongly supported by the Jewish initiative *Meshulash* (in English: "triangle"). This group was founded in 1991 and is mostly made up of Jews who have chosen to live in Berlin. *Meshulash* makes artistic and political statements on German memorial policies.

OTTO WEIDT FORMER WORKSHOP FOR THE BLIND

Rosenthaler Strasse 39 back courtyard (Mitte)
Open: Monday–Friday noon–8 pm, Saturday and Sunday 11 am–8 pm

Otto Weidt (1883–1948) had his broom and brush factory in the left wing of the first floor of the building in the first back courtyard at Rosenthaler Strasse 39. During National Socialism, he employed Jewish forced laborers, both male and female, most of whom were blind or deaf-mute. After the war began, he produced goods for the Wehrmacht and his factory was classified as crucial to the war effort.

He helped at least fifty-six Jews either by employing or hiding them, by supplying false identity papers and food, and by repeatedly bribing the Gestapo and the Employment Office. In the autumn of 1942, he even managed to get a group of blind and deaf-mute Jews released who had been arrested at his workshop by the Gestapo and taken to a collection camp on Grosse Hamburger Strasse. He rented storage rooms on Brücken- and Grossbeerenstrasse and set up a hiding place for the families of his workers. But most of them were later denounced, discovered and deported to concentration camps. A total of twenty-seven survivors owe their lives to Otto Weidt. After the war he worked for the reconstruction of a Jewish community home for the elderly in Pankow-Niederschönhausen.

As early as 1947 Weidt publicly demanded that a memorial dedicated to the Jews who had been murdered be built in a public place in Berlin. He died impoverished and embittered in 1948.

It was only in 1994 that a tomb of honor was erected at his gravesite in the city cemetery on Onkel-Tom-Strasse in Berlin-Zehlendorf. The exhibition "Blind Faith" that was organized by students in the rooms of the former workshop received such positive attention that it was made a permanent establishment. Since the beginning of 2001 the workshop exhibit is a branch of the Berlin Jewish Museum. The entrance ticket to the museum is also valid for the workshop on the same and following day. In September 1999 a memorial plaque was set on the ground of the courtyard to commemorate Weidt.

PLACE OF REMEMBRANCE IN THE BAYERISCHES VIERTEL (SCHÖNEBERG)

The neighborhood around the Bayerischer Platz was popularly called the Jewish Switzerland due to the large number of prosperous Jewish residents living there. Some 6,000 Jews were deported just from this neighborhood. The original installation by **Renata Stih** and **Frieder Schnock**, set up in June 1993 successfully illustrates the daily dimensions of the National Socialist exclusion and extermination policies towards Jewish citizens. Eighty white signs have been hung on street masts. On one side a brief quote from a National Socialist anti-Jewish decree, law or journal entry is cited with the corresponding date. On the other side a pictogram illustrates the text. The uncommented, short sentences state for example, that "Jews are to be expelled from sports and gymnastic clubs." (April 25, 1933).

Just after the signs were hung citizens went to the police to report what they believed was an antisemitic provocation. The state security agency responsible for those kinds of crimes was informed and had the installation removed. Eventually permission was granted to have the signs hung again. A small panel was hung beneath the signs to explain the memorial project. Two maps have been set up to provide an overview of the locations of each sign – one is at the Bayerischer Platz and the other is in front of the entrance portal to the Schöneberg town hall.

STUMBLING STONES

For information: Kreuzberg Museum, Adalbertstraße 95A (Kreuzberg), Tel. 50 58 52 33

Cobblestones with a brass slate providing names and biographical dates are set into the sidewalks at sites where Jews, Sinti and Roma, homosexuals, handicapped, resistance fighters and Jehovah's Witnesses who were murdered by the National Socialists once lived. The sculptor **Gunter Demnig** from Cologne initiated this project together with the Berlin New Society for the Arts ("Neue Gesellschaft für Bildende Kunst") in 1996. This memorial work gives the victims at least their names back, and their lives, through the biographical dates placed where they once lived, are pulled out of the anonymity of statistics. In a school project, enthusiastic children rummage through the available files and documents in their research on people who fell victim to National Socialist extermination policies. They visit the past places of residence, speak with the current residents and even conduct interviews with people who lived through the time. Over 400 stumbling stones have been donated already. Many can be seen around Hackescher Markt and Oranienburger Strasse. A donation of ninety-five Euro is requested to sponsor a stone.

TOPOGRAPHY OF TERROR

Niederkirchnerstrasse 8 (Kreuzberg), Tel. 25 48 67 03
Open: daily 10 am–6 pm in winter, 10 am–8 pm in summer

The Topography of Terror Foundation was founded in 1992 to document the events at an authentic site of National Socialist crimes. During National Socialism the most important institutions of terror were located on these grounds. This is where the headquarters of the Secret State Police, the SS Reich leadership, the Security of the SS and as of 1939, the Reich Security Main Office were located. The people responsible for the National Socialist mass crimes, like Himmler, Heydrich and Kaltenbrunner, had their offices here. And the Gestapo set up a detainment prison here for very important prisoners. The buildings, which were severely damaged in World War II, were torn down after the war. Not until 1987 was a decision made to establish a temporary exhibition hall to present the history of this site.

The planned new building, an exhibition building designed by the Swiss architect Peter Zumthor, was delayed for years and in the end was not built. Since the building costs threatened to exceed well beyond the planned budget, construction was discontinued and the staircase towers that were erected in late 2004 were torn down again. An exhibition is currently on view along the excavated cellar ruins on Niederkirchnerstrasse.

WANNSEE CONFERENCE HOUSE MEMORIAL

Am Grossen Wannsee 56–58 (Zehlendorf), Tel. 805 00 10
Open: Monday–Friday 10 am–6 pm, Saturday and Sunday 2 pm–6 pm

At Grosser Wannsee, an idyllic area immersed in nature and one of Berlin's most beautiful and expensive residential neighborhoods, there is a site associated with the largest genocide in the history of mankind. On January 20, 1942, the notorious Wannsee Conference convened in the fashionable Villa Minoux. Undersecretaries of various Reich ministries and high level SS leaders attended the meeting to discuss the details of what was called the "Final Solution to the Jewish Question." Reinhard Heydrich, head of the Security Police and the Security Service chaired the meeting. Its protocol, written by Adolf Eichmann, the head of the Office of Jewish Affairs, was discovered by American investigators in 1947 beneath a pile of files that had been left behind in the Foreign Office. When the Wannsee Conference took place, the mass murder of Jews was already well underway. It is often mistakenly assumed the "Final Solution" was resolved at this meeting. In fact, organization and technical details were agreed upon and more people were informed of and involved in the operation. In her book on the trial of Adolf Eichmann, Hannah Arendt characterizes this inhuman bureaucracy of administrative killers as the "banality of evil."

The memorial opened in 1992, fifty years after the Wannsee Conference. A permanent exhibition is on display in more than ten rooms. It documents the history of exclusion, expulsion, deportation and extermination of German Jews and later other European Jews. The building also houses an educational center opened to school classes, an archive, library and media library.

"WOMEN'S BLOCK" MONUMENT FOR THE WOMEN'S PROTEST IN THE ROSENSTRASSE

Rosenstrasse 2–4 (Mitte)

The sculptor **Ingeborg Hunzinger** created the solid, red sandstone sculpture with human figures and Jewish symbols. In 1988 the city of East Berlin commissioned her to create a monument of anti-fascist resistance. She chose the women's protest against what is known as the "Factory Action." The monument that was taken over by the Berlin Senate after reunification was not inaugurated until October 18, 1995.

In early 1943, some 27,000 Jews still lived in Berlin – most of them worked as forced laborers in factories considered crucial to the war effort. Some of them lived in so-called "mixed marriages." According to National Socialist legislation, this term referred to marriages between Jews and so-called "Aryans." On February 27, 1943, the SS rounded up some 7,000 Jews at their places of work in preparation for deportation to Auschwitz. Most of the men, who lived in what was referred to as a "privileged marriage," were initially detained in the former Jewish Community Welfare Office at Rosenstrasse 2–4.

From February 28 to March 11, several hundred wives and mothers, but also other relatives and passersby, protested on Rosenstrasse, calling for the release of their imprisoned husbands and sons. They were not politically organized and acted spontaneously and non-violently, out of pure desperation. Due to the massive Allied bombings of Berlin on the night of March 1st and the heavy losses at the East Front, the National Socialist leadership worried that the general mood of the Berlin population might turn against them. In order to avoid adding fuel to the flames, Goebbels called for the release of the prisoners, even the twenty-five who had already been sent to Auschwitz.

The most recent research conducted at the Center for Antisemitism Research at the Technische Universität Berlin, however, has found that the men imprisoned at Rosenstrasse were not going to be deported after all. They were to take on responsibility for the administration of the remaining community members and other similar tasks. Given this knowledge, the women's protest did not cause their husbands' release, as was previously believed, but it still remains what is sadly a rare example of civil disobedience from Germans during the Nazi era.

In 1993, two pillars were erected on both sides of the grassy area off of Rosenstrasse to inform visitors of the events that occurred here. The idea came from students of the College for Social Work and Pedagogy who had already erected a column in 1992. Margarethe von Trotta's award-winning film "Rosenstrasse" about the women's protest was an international success in 2003.

Cultural Institutions and Events

PAST AND PRESENT JEWISH CULTURE IN BERLIN

The Jewish residents of Berlin had an impressive influence on the civil culture of this city. The historical division of 1933 put an end not only to the marked presence of Jewish life in Berlin – it meant a complete end to the cultural life that Jews had strongly contributed to.

The long list of important Jewish writers, publishers, patrons, philosophers and artists reads like a "who's who" of Berlin history. The circle of friends acquainted with Moses Mendelssohn – without question the most significant authors and philosophers of the time – marks the beginning of this trend. The literary salons of the baptized Jewish women Dorothea Schlegel, Henriette Herz and Rahel von Varnhagen drew the intellectual elite of the Prussian capital together and gave them a home to discuss their ideas. Berlin politicians such as Eduard Lasker (1829–1884), Ludwig Bamberger (1823–1899) and Ferdinand Lassalle (1825–1864) were significantly responsible for establishing a political culture of liberalism and tolerance in 19th century Germany. Generous patrons such as James Henry Simon and Eduard Arnhold (1849–1929) donated their precious collections to the city's museums. Financially successful entrepreneurs like Josef Garbáty-Rosenthal (1851–1939) and Moritz Manheimer showed themselves to be selfless supporters of social institutions. Artists and authors were always welcome to enjoy the high quality book and art collections housed in the tasteful villas of such prominent figures as Samuel Fischer and Walther Rathenau. The families of Mendelssohn, Ullstein, Mosse, Tietz and Wertheim, just to name a few, were for generations closely connected to Berlin until the National Socialists brutally ended this tradition through expulsion, disfranchisement and murder.

The ascendancy of German literature and art from the beginning of the 19th century to the early 1930s is mostly due to those writers and artists who were reduced to their Jewish origins by the National Socialists. Having achieved civil equality, many Jewish artists regarded themselves above all as German. Some of them left the Jewish congregation; others showed a lifelong commitment to the concerns of the Jewish community. Most Jews were highly assimilated and identified with German culture, the German people and the German state. But anti-Semites, racists and National Socialists continually succeeded in indiscriminately denying this very diverse minority its German identity, declaring them all to be merely "Jews." Only after the Jews were excluded from society and ultimately annihilated did it become clear how important they had been and what a great loss their absence was to German society.

Event locations, dates and programs of current Jewish cultural events can be found in the daily newspapers, various city magazines and on the Internet (www.jewish-berlin-online.com and www.hagalil.com/deutschland/berlin and www.berlin-judentum.de).

BAMAH – JEWISH THEATER AT STEINPLATZ

Hardenbergstraße 12 (Charlottenburg), Tel. 251 10 96
Performance: always at 8 pm

Since May 26, 2001 the Jewish Bamah theater performs works by Israeli, German and international contemporary authors. Their diverse program also includes readings of works by Jewish authors such as Isaac Bashevis Singer, songs by Friedrich Hollaender and Georg Kreisler and even celebrations of traditional Jewish holidays and the weekly Sabbath evening. *Bamah* means "stage" in Hebrew. The Israeli **Dan Lahav**, who has lived in Berlin since 1981 and used to direct the Jewish Culture Days, now enthusiastically directs the ambitious theater in the tradition of popular Jewish Theater as it existed in Berlin before 1933. The Off-Theater, which manages without public subsidies, was first located in the Bürgerhaus of Charlottenburg-Wilmersdorf. Since October 2004 Bamah has been housed in the old "Filmbühne am Steinplatz" that was once a 120 seat moviehouse. The stage on which the nine actors perform is therefore relatively narrow. There is also a theater café which serves Jewish-Israeli specialties.

FORMER JEWISH MUSEUM

Oranienburger Strasse 31 (Mitte)

When an exhibition on Jewish art and antiquities was shown in London in 1906, the Berlin Association for the Support of Jewish Art decided to engage in something similar. The Jewish Artists Exhibition opened in the Gallery for Old and New Art at Wilhelmstrasse 45 in 1908 and was the first of its kind in Berlin.

The Dresden Jeweler **Albert Wolf** (1841–1907) had already donated his large collection of Judaica to the Berlin Jewish community in 1905. But it wasn't until February 18, 1917 that the Art Collection of the Berlin Jewish community (Wolf Foundation) could be shown to the public for the first time in the community's administration building on Oranienburger Strasse 29. **Moritz Stern** (1864–1939), the head librarian and director of the Jewish Community Library, looked after the expanding collection after Wolf's death. Palestinian antiquities, antique Jewish coins, medals of Jewish interest, seals and ritual objects, portraits of important Jewish figures, handwriting, prints and books were on display, but after thieves stole valuable pieces in 1923, the exhibit was forced to close. The art historian **Karl Schwarz** (1885–1962) took over direction of the art collection in 1930. Just before, on November 28, 1929, the Jewish Museum Association was founded with the aim to open a Jewish museum. The renowned painter and president of the Academy of Arts, **Max Liebermann**, agreed to serve as honorary chairman of the association. A few years later he donated a self-portrait to the museum for its opening.

The Community Board made the first floor of the building on Oranienburger Strasse 31 available for the museum exhibition. The building that had been donated by Bertha und Moritz Manheimer in 1896 used to be the infirmary of the Jewish community. After the community's house architect **Alexander Beer** converted the space into an exhibition room, the Jewish Museum opened on January 24, 1933, just days before Hitler's seizure of power.

After Schwarz immigrated to Tel Aviv that same year, **Erna Stein** (1903–1983) took over his position until she left for Palestine two years later. **Franz Landsberger** (1883–1964), who had been a professor of art history at the Breslau University until 1933, became the museum's new director. One of the exhibitions produced under the oppressive atmosphere of the Nazi era was the Max Liebermann memorial exhibit that opened in February 1936, one year after his death. Landsberger was among the many arrested during the November pogrom of 1938 and interned in Sachsenhausen. Friends of his living abroad were able to intervene and achieve his release, after which he immigrated to the United States via England. The museum was forced to close and many pieces of the precious collection were irretrievably lost in the following years. The Jewish Gallery is today located in the building's basement.

HACKESCHES HOFTHEATER

Rosenthaler Strasse 40 (Mitte), Tel. 283 25 87

The Hackesche Höfe is one of the new public attractions in Berlin. The eight differently designed inner courtyards run from Rosenthaler Strasse to Sophienstrasse. The courtyard complex with its successful mix of living, working and entertainment space was built in 1906–1907 according to plans by **Kurt Berndt**. The Hackesches Hoftheater is located in the second courtyard and invites audiences almost every evening to enjoy concerts with Yiddish songs or Klezmer music. Interpreters of Yiddish, Ashkenazi and Sephardic songs, such as Jalda Rebling, Inna, Mark Aizikovitch, Kerstin Kozubek and Karsten Troyke – as well as Klezmer groups like Aufwind, Grinsteins Mischpoche and Harry's Freilach, perform here regularly. In the small black room small tables and chairs are set up in front of the stage and further back, rows of seats have been lined up on a ramp. The bar in the foyer serves beverages.

Grinsteins Mischpoche at Hackesches Hoftheater

Jewish Museum of Berlin

JEWISH CULTURE DAYS

The Jewish Culture Days take place in November. This cultural marathon runs under a different theme each year, presenting concerts, theater presentations and readings. The Gesher Theater from Tel Aviv, founded by Jewish actors from the former Soviet Union, has delighted many audiences. Israeli stars such as Chava Alberstein and David Broza have also been applauded here in the past. The extensive program also includes a number of lectures, podium discussions and films.

JEWISH CULTURE SOCIETY

Oranienburger Strasse 26 (Entrance at Krausnickstrasse; Mitte),
Tel. 282 66 69 or 28 59 80 52
Open: Monday–Thursday 11 am–5 pm, Friday 11 am–2 pm

In addition to the very small official Jewish community in East Berlin, there were a number of unregistered Jews living in the GDR, most of whom were completely assimilated and non-religious. Many of them chose to live there because they believed in communist ideals and maintained an anti-fascist mentality. Especially the children and grandchildren of parents who represented the interests of the state rediscovered their forgotten Jewish roots after having been disappointed in socialism as it had been realized in the GDR. They cautiously made contact with the Jewish community, without becoming religious active members.

The Jewish Culture Society that was founded in 1990 is an example of this kind of private group of secular, even atheist, intellectuals of Jewish descent. Its members hope to enrich their cultural identity with Jewish tradition. The society hosts alternative Sabbath services every Friday evening and holds readings of Jewish authors and lectures on topics relating to Judaism. It also works towards the integration of Russian Jews. Its newsletter, *Jüdische Korrespondenz*, is published monthly.

The club is legally independent from the official Jewish community, but maintains informal contact to it.

JEWISH GALLERY

Oranienburger Strasse 31 (Mitte), Tel. 282 86 23
Open: Monday–Thursday 10 am to 6 pm, Friday 10 am to 5 pm,
Sunday 11 am to 3 pm

The Jewish Gallery, which was founded in 1993 by the Central Welfare Office of Jews in Germany, exhibits mostly Jewish artists from the
former Soviet Union. Crafts, posters and postcards are also on sale. The
gallery re-opened in 2001 after being renovated. Some of the many
artists that have already exhibited their work include Anatoli Tanel
from Charkow, Tatyana Sklyar from Odessa and Anatoli Kaplan from
St. Petersburg.

JEWISH MUSEUM OF BERLIN

Lindenstrasse 9–14 (Kreuzberg), Tel. 25 99 33 00,
tours: 25 99 33 05
Open: Monday 10 am–10 pm, Tuesday–Sunday 10 am–8 pm, closed
only on the Jewish High Holy Days Rosh Hashanah and Yom Kippur
and on December 24

In 1971, in connection with the exhibition "Achievements and Fates"
in the Berlin City Museum that opened in honor of the 300th anniversary of the founding of the Berlin Jewish community, the idea of establishing a new Jewish museum in Berlin emerged. In 1975 the association "Friends of the Jewish Museum" began working towards this goal
by establishing a new collection. The results of this effort were dem-
onstrated by the opening of a Jewish Department in the city museum.
The three-winged baroque building of the former "Königliches Colle-
gienhaus" was built from 1734 to 1735 based on a design by **Philipp
Gerlach**. This was originally the seat of the imperial supreme court. After World War I the Consistorium of the Protestant Church of Brandenburg moved in. The building was heavily damaged by an air-raid in
February 1945 and not rebuilt until the sixties. The newly founded
City Museum of Berlin (West) established itself here.

An international competition for an addition to the Berlin City Museum with an enlarged Jewish museum division took place in 1988. The Jewish department that was busting at its seams was housed on the top floor of the Martin Gropius Building on Niederkirchnerstrasse at the time.

First prize was awarded on June 23, 1989 to the design titled "Between the Lines" by the architect **Daniel Libeskind**. Libeskind was born in 1946 in Lodz, Poland. After completing his degree in architecture in the United States and Great Britain, he taught at various academic institutions. He is one of the best known deconstructionalists along with Peter Eisenman, Frank O. Gehry, Zaha Hadid and the architecture office Coop/Himmelb(l)au. This school radically questions traditional architectural language by, for example, strongly avoiding right-wing angles and by seemingly discarding the laws of structural engineering. The symbolic foundation stone was laid on November 9, 1992 and the actual building construction began in March of the following year. In January 1999, after six years of construction, the building was finally opened to the public. Hundreds of ecstatic people poured into the still empty building for the first time on the "Long Night of Museums." Following this initial success, tours were offered regularly beginning in February 1999. Over one and a half years, more than 230,000 people took advantage of the opportunity to marvel at the still unfurnished museum. Empty, the space conveyed an immediate impression of the sculptural and symbolic architecture of the building.

From a bird's eye view the five floor building looks like a bolt of lightning. The exterior walls are clad in silver-gray zinc; the narrow angular window slits are arranged irregularly. Voids traverse the building's longitudinal axis. They symbolize all that was lost as a result of the annihilation of Jews during the period of National Socialism. A striking outdoor area is the E. T. A. Hoffmann Garden. This consists of forty-nine oversized slanted concrete steles that slightly resemble Peter Eisenman's memorial design, only here there are trees growing out of them. The garden is named after E. T. A. Hoffmann (1776–1822), not because he had a Jewish background, but because he served as supreme court councilor in the building next door that later became the City Museum. The irregularly cobbled Paul Celan Courtyard is set between the two wings of the Libeskind building and faces the older building.

The new building is connected by an underground staircase to the old City Musuem, where the museum entrance is located. In the new building, visitors first arrive at an intersection of three axes. From the Axis of Exile, which symbolizes the exodus of German Jews from their homeland, visitors are led out of the museum and into the E. T. A. Hoffmann Garden. The Holocaust Axis is a dead end, leading to the empty shaft-like Holocaust Tower built of bare, exposed concrete. The central axis leads to a long, steep staircase that connects the different levels. The floor of the museum's lower level is slanted, an effect intended to disturb visitors' sense of balance as they wander through the museum. This detail is reinforced by asymmetrical rooms with sharp angles and crooked walls.

The many years of quarreling over the status of the museum led the museum's first director **Amnon Barzel** to resign from his position in 1994. In 1997, former US Secretary of Treasury **Michael Blumenthal** was brought in as the new director, which due to his diplomatic skills was soon regarded as a stroke of luck. Blumenthal, whose family came from Berlin, has meanwhile written a very interesting and personal book on German-Jewish history.

It was difficult to find enough artifacts to fill the 4,500 square meters of exhibition space. A solution was found in the currently popular concept of a narrative museum, which uses multimedia presentations and replicas of original documents to show the diverse history of Jews in Germany.

A tour through the museum goes through thirteen segments covering two thousand years of German-Jewish history. Some of the most spectacular artifacts on display include original hand-written medieval texts, the Torah curtain donated by Moses Mendelssohn and his wife Fromet and the self-portrait by Felix Nussbaum. The museum had already welcomed its 500,000th visitor to the exhibit by early May 2002.

Through a partnership with the New York Leo Baeck Institute, the museum hopes also to establish itself as a scholarly center of German-Jewish studies. A library with this focus is currently being developed.

JEWISH STREET FESTIVAL ON ORANIENBURGER STRASSE (KREUZBERG)

Since 1997, the Jewish street festival has been held each year in June on Oranienburger Strasse. The first festival was organized to celebrate the thirtieth anniversary of the reunification of Jerusalem in 1967. There were strong protests at the time from Palestinians who saw no reason to celebrate this anniversary.

Jewish musicians perform concerts on an outdoor stage. Different stands are set up along the street offering Israeli snacks, jewelry, souvenirs and books on Jewish topics. Some stands provide information on Jewish organizations or collect financial donations.

NEW SYNAGOGUE OF BERLIN – CENTRUM JUDAICUM FOUNDATION

Oranienburger Strasse 29 (Mitte), Tel. 284 01–250
Open: Sunday–Thursday 10 am–5:30 pm, Friday 10 am–1:30 pm

(See page 26)

Jewish Restaurants and Shops

BÄCKEREI KÄDTLER (BAKERY)

Danziger Strasse 135 (Prenzlauer Berg), Tel. 423 32 33
Kastanienallee 88 (Prenzlauer Berg), Tel. 449 32 14
Open: Monday–Friday 6 am–6:30 pm, Saturday 7 am–noon

The only kosher bakery in Berlin is run by a long-established Berlin bakery. Different breads including the Sabbath bread *(Hallah)*, rolls and cake are prepared and sold strictly in accordance with the Jewish dietary laws. It delivers to Jewish community institutions as well as to Café Bleibergs. From an orthodox viewpoint, however, the fact that sausage (including pork sausage) is also sold and consumed there is dubious.

BÄCKEREI TAITLER (CAFÉ)

Dahlmannstrasse 22 (Charlottenburg), Tel. 31 80 81 09
Open: Sunday–Thursday 9 am–8 pm, Friday until Sabbath begins

Baruch Teidler opened this cafe in May 2004. The name goes back to the correct spelling of the family name that was Germanized after the war by German authorities. The delicious baked goods are produced daily by the Israeli pastry chef Yair Perez. Freshly baked Sabbath bread (*Hallah*) is sold every Friday. Breakfast is served after 9 am and various snacks such as borekas and bagels, coffee, Israeli wine and beer can also be ordered. The catering service can be hired for private occasions.

BETH CAFÉ

Tucholskystrasse 40 (Mitte), Tel. 281 31 35
Open: Sunday–Thursday noon–8 pm

The *Beth* Café, run by the strictly religious Adass Yisroel congregation, is a kosher establishment. The Hebrew word *Beth* simply means
"house." A *Beth* Café is thus a café (house). It was opened in 1991 in
the unrenovated old and now new independent orthodox community
center. Israeli snacks such as falafel, bagel, salad and soup are served
along with coffee, tea and cold beverages. There are also a number of
vegetarian dishes on the menu. In summer, guests can sit in the outdoor garden courtyard.

BLEIBERGS (CAFÉ)

Nürnberger Strasse 45a (Schöneberg), Tel. 21 92 36 24
Open: Sunday–Thursday 11 am–9 pm, Friday 9 am–3 pm (summer),
9 am–noon (winter); closed on Jewish holidays

The small Café Bleibergs was established in May 2004 and offers coffee, wine, cake and small snacks. The kosher Kädtler bakery delivers
fresh baked goods here daily. This cozy café can also be rented for private occasions. Trips to Israel can be booked in the Manuela Hoffmann travel agency located in the same building.

GABRIEL'S (RESTAURANT)

Fasanenstrasse 79–80 (Charlottenburg), Tel. 882 61 38
Open: Sunday–Friday 11:30 am–3:30 pm and 6:30 pm–11 pm,
Saturday 11:30 am–3:30 pm

The oldest Jewish restaurant in Berlin serving kosher food is located
on the first floor of the Jewish community center. Gabriel's used to be
called "Arche Noah." Its white tablecloths and old fashioned decor

Beth Café

Salomon Bagels

conveys a 1970s atmosphere. The menu of this quite small restaurant offers various meat, poultry and fish dishes prepared in the tradition of Jewish and Israeli cooking. The prices are moderate. Every Tuesday Gabriel's offers a buffet with over thirty different dishes for eighteen Euro.

KOL BO (GROCERIES)

Auguststrasse 77–78 (Mitte), Tel. 281 31 35
Open: Monday–Thursday 2 pm–6 pm, Friday 10:30 am–2:30 pm

The Adass Yisroel orthodox congregation has run this shop, which offers a surprisingly large selection of kosher food and wine, since 1992. The Hebrew word *Kol Bo* means "everything inside." The community center of Adass Yisroel is right around the corner on Tucholskystrasse. The products come from both Israel and France and the baked goods are homemade. But the shop also sells books on Jewish subjects, calendars, souvenirs, Sabbath candles, ice cream, Israeli cosmetics and religious objects.

KOSHER DELI (GROCERIES)

Goethestrasse 61 (Charlottenburg), Tel. 31 50 92 43
Open: Monday–Thursday 9:30 am–5 pm, Friday 9 am–2:30 pm

This kosher store attracts attention with its tastefully decorated window display and a store sign in German and Hebrew lettering. The interior is very light and orderly. Customers can serve themselves from shelves stocked with food products and Israeli wine. There is also a freezer filled with veal, sausages and turkey. Behind the counter freshly prepared dishes including salads (Hummus, eggplant, Tahini and red beets just to name a few), meat, sausage and fresh vegetables are available. Sabbath candles, Israeli snacks, *Matzah* and olives are also sold. The hand-shaped *Hamsa* amulet on the wall is the only decorative object in the store.

KOSHERIA (WINE)

Kantstrasse 141 (Charlottenburg), Tel. 31 99 26 75
Open: Monday–Friday 8:30 am–8 pm, Saturday 10:30 am–5 pm

This wine store that opened in November 2004 sells a unique selection of kosher wine from all over the world. Kosher wine does not contain any supplementary ingredients like sugar, sulfur or yeast. Customers may taste the wines or drink an espresso at the small bar. CDs of the young cantor Avitall Gerstetter can also be purchased.

LIEBERMANNS (RESTAURANT)

Lindenstrasse 9–14 (Kreuzberg), Tel. 25 93 97 60
Open: daily 9:30 am–11 pm

Liebermanns restaurant and café in the Jewish Museum of Berlin is located in the left wing of the old building, the former "Kollegienhaus." Its seats about one hundred guests in three differently arranged rooms. The "free flow restaurant" is dominated by a self-service counter that becomes a cocktail bar after 6 pm. The "A-la-carte restaurant" and next door "atrium" with a view out to the courtyard offer dining in a tasteful ambience.

The young Israeli chef Eran Harel is responsible for the international kosher-style Jewish cooking. Pork and shellfish are not served. Some of the house specialties include chopped chicken liver on caramelized sliced apples, borscht, lamb cutlet with tabouli salad and baked silver bream filet. It is also possible to order strictly kosher dishes. Groups can order breakfast before they visit the museum. A formal Sabbath dinner is offered every Friday, for which reservations should be made in advance.

LITERATURHANDLUNG (BOOKS)

Joachimstaler Strasse 13 (Charlottenburg), Tel. 882 42 50
Open: Monday–Friday 9:30 am–6:30 pm, Saturday 9:30 am–2 pm

This bookstore specializing in Jewish authors and books on Jewish subjects is located in a sunny and spacious shop. The police presence outside the entrance is both for the shop and for the community institutions that are housed in the same building complex. Rachel Salamander, the store manager, also runs a Jewish literature bookstore in Munich and Vienna and publishes a catalogue with thirty-two subject areas and 7,000 book titles by Jewish authors. The excellently stocked shop is one of a kind in Berlin, offering both new publications and older works that are still in print. The large selection of literature covers fiction, second-hand and new books, Yiddish literature, German and English specialist books on Jewish history, culture, Kabbalah and philosophy. It also carries language guides, dictionaries, travel guides and selected religious literature in Hebrew, such as the Bible, Mishnah, Talmud and prayer books. A small selection of CDs and tapes with synagogal and Klezmer music is also available.

PLÄZL (GROCERIES)

Passauer Strasse 4 (Schöneberg), Tel. 217 75 06
Open: Monday–Thursday 9 am–6 pm, Friday 9 am–1:30 pm

The kosher shop Pläzl is located close to the famous KaDeWe department store and with the Star of David and Hebrew lettering in the shop window is easy to find. The store sells mostly kosher food imported from Israel. It is stocked with a wide range of products – from ready-to-serve meals to fish and sweets. The tiled floor is decorated with a Star of David. In the connecting room there is a large selection of Israeli wines and spirits.

SALOMON BAGELS

Joachimstaler Strasse 13 (Charlottenburg), Tel. 821 04 04
Potsdamer-Platz-Arkaden (Tiergarten), Tel. 25 29 76 26
Open: Monday–Friday 9 am–8 pm, Saturday 9 am–4 pm

As the name suggests, Salomon Bagels sells mostly bagels. It offers many different kinds of fresh bagels as well as a wide selection of salads and spreads.

The two branches of Salomon Bagels couldn't be more different. The store on Joachimstaler Strasse is situated in a building complex alongside the Jewish literature bookstore, a synagogue and various community institutions. That explains the permanent police presence in front. Although it is close to the busy Kurfürstendamm boulevard, not as many people stumble upon the store as might be expected. It is quite small and simply furnished.

The branch in the indoor arcade at Potdamer Platz offers a very different atmosphere. The cafe is situated on the upper level of the veritable shopping mall that unfortunately was erected overnight in a not very original design. A broad selection of delicacies on display behind the glass counter draw in lots of shoppers from the busy mall.

SCHALOM (GROCERIES)

Wielandstrasse 43 (Charlottenburg), Tel. 312 11 31
Open: Monday–Friday 11 am–5 pm

This kosher store exists since 1965 and is the oldest of its kind in Berlin. A sign over the driveway draws attention to the small shop in the back courtyard. Customers at Schalom, which offers a wide range of Israeli specialties, are served with the friendliness of a mom-and-pop corner shop. The store has a number of Carmel, Golan and Yarden wines and many different kinds of champagnes and spirits including Sabra liqueur. Among the diverse foods offered is Halva, a Middle-Eastern sweet, and kosher chocolate from Switzerland. Frozen chicken, turkey and sausages can be found in the freezer.

TABULARIUM (TOYS, BOOKS, MUSIC, RELIGIOUS RITUAL OBJECTS)

Krausnickstrasse 23 (Mitte), Tel. 280 82 03
Open: Monday–Saturday 11 am–7 pm

The Latin word "Tabularium" actually refers to a document collection or an archive. This store sells a very diverse selection of products. About half the space is filled with carefully selected toys and souvenirs. There are also German and English-language publications on Jewish topics, especially works on local Jewish history, and books by Jewish authors. Tapes and CDs of synagogal, Klezmer and Israeli pop music are also on sale. There is a wide selection of board games, especially backgammon, and dice games with biblical and Israeli motives. Various religious ritual objects are also on sale such as Sabbath candleholders, *Kiddush* cups, *Mezuzot* and *Kippahs*. The shop carries a small selection of kosher wines and spirits as well as Israeli "Ahavah" cosmetics.

Index of Persons